The World's Greatest Truths

A Gift For You...

This book
of
The World's Greatest Truths
is presented as a special gift to

_____

from

_____

The World's Greatest Truths

JAMES BRAMLETT

CREATIVE PUBLISHERS
Virginia Beach, Virginia

Copyright ©1988 by James D. Bramlett

*This is a Creative book
published by*

Creative Publishers
P. O. Box 61431
Virginia Beach, Virginia 23462

Library of Congress Catalog Card Number 88-070056

Bramlett, James
The World's Greatest Truths
ISBN 0-945-64206-7

All rights reserved. No part of this publication may be reproduced, stored in a retrieval system, or transmitted in any form or by any means—electronic, mechanical, photocopy, recording, or any other—except for brief quotations in printed reviews, without the prior permission of the publisher.

Scripture quotations are from various translations of the Bible. See "Notes" for specific references and also for style comment on the capitalizaton of pronouns relating to deity.

Printed in the United States of America

Dedication

This book is dedicated to:

*Becky and Michelle
and other offspring
already loved but yet unborn…*

*New life looks around
at sight and sound
and wonders.
"What does it all mean?"
most eventually say.
Some may never know.
But you will.
And others, too, I pray.*

Table of Contents

Prologue		13
Introduction		17
Chapter 1	THE WORLD'S GREATEST BOOK	21
	One Minute Summary	32
Chapter 2	THE WORLD'S GREATEST PERSON	35
	One Minute Summary	46
Chapter 3	THE WORLD'S GREATEST SECRET	47
	One Minute Summary	55
Chapter 4	THE WORLD'S GREATEST SUBSTANCE	57
	One Minute Summary	71
Chapter 5	THE WORLD'S GREATEST NAME	73
	One Minute Summary	84
Chapter 6	THE WORLD'S GREATEST MESSAGE	87
	One Minute Summary	95
Chapter 7	THE WORLD'S GREATEST EXPERIENCE	97
	One Minute Summary	106
Chapter 8	THE WORLD'S GREATEST LIFE	107
	One Minute Summary	116
Chapter 9	THE WORLD'S GREATEST HOPE	117
	One Minute Summary	126
Chapter 10	THE WORLD'S GREATEST PRIVILEGE	129
	One Minute Summary	137
Chapter 11	THE WORLD'S GREATEST OBLIGATION	139
	One Minute Summary	151

Chapter 12	THE WORLD'S GREATEST CONFLICT	155
	One Minute Summary	161
Appendix I	THE WORLD'S GREATEST QUESTIONS with *One Minute Answers*	163
Appendix II	THE WORLD'S MOST MYSTERIOUS DISAPPEARANCE, *Solved in One Minute!*	181
Epilogue		187
Notes		191

Prologue

This book contains the basic and essential truths that *every* human being should know. Without a doubt, they are really "the world's greatest truths." If you are a human being, you definitely should know them.

All these truths share one amazing trait—*simplicity*. The average person can read about 200 to 250 words in one minute. Surprisingly, the average person can read, understand and, where appropriate, act upon each of the world's greatest truths in about one minute or less! Accordingly, each chapter has a One Minute Summary in case you are really in a hurry, and for quick reviews. In addition, Appendix I contains One Minute Answers to "the world's greatest questions."

The One Minute concept in this book is revolutionary, yet thousands of years old. It proves anew that the deepest and most profound truths in the world can be quickly communicated and understood. Of course, it takes a little longer to explain why they are true and how they work, which each chapter does. But you will enjoy the explanations, which are surely worth a few extra minutes of your time.

Just knowing these truths will make you wise, actually wiser than many highly educated people. By reading and understanding these truths, you will attain the highest level of intellectual awareness of the meaning of life.

The information in this small book has been described as more valuable than "choice gold."[1] It can benefit you daily for your entire life, and even afterwards. Sound incredible? But it's true.

These may be the most important few minutes you will ever spend.

ENJOY!

Acknowledgments

Special appreciation is extended to:

Mark W. Wilson, M.A.,, for his assistance in editing and input on some of the technical areas.

Robert A. McDonough, President of McDonough Media, Chesapeake, Virginia, for his valuable assistance and recommendations.

The hundreds of diligent and faithful scholars whose study and conclusions have shed light on these "greatest truths."

Those friends with whom I shared the concept and need for this book, and who caught the vision with me. The vision "will not tarry."

Last but not least, my dear wife, Mary Ann, who not only tolerates my endless bleary-eyed hours in front of the "green screen" (word processor), but is always encouraging.

Introduction

Here's a shocking story I once read that dramatically affected my life:

> "Several years ago there was a politician who was a very busy person. He was so busy that he didn't even have a minute to spare. He was really busy. One day he was rushing out of a meeting and on his way to another meeting when a newspaper reporter approached him. 'Excuse me, sir,' the reporter asked, 'can you spare just one minute?'
>
> "The politician hurriedly replied, 'Sorry, but I couldn't spare one minute for Jesus Christ right now.'
>
> "Just a minute later he was assassinated."

End of story? Unfortunately not. The politician suddenly found himself in eternity, with all the time in the world, and then some—actually, forever. Frankly, that's always bothered me. He said he could not even spare one minute for Jesus Christ and he may be out there in eternity somewhere, alone, without Christ. It's really scary when you stop to think about it.

This story did get me to thinking. It made me realize that modern people are incredibly busy. We don't have time for anything. It's always rush, rush, rush. "Almost nobody, it seems, has enough time," said a front-page newspaper article from a nationwide New York Times News Service wire.[1] And it's the supersonic age. We don't always know where we are going, but we're in a hurry to get there.

Because we are so busy and in such a hurry, we must have an "instant" everything: instant coffee, instant breakfast, TV dinners, microwave meals, quick weight loss, instant car washes, jiffy lubes, instant credit, "crash" courses, ad infinitum.

There must be a divinely ordained division of time—One Minute—because that's what everything seems to take. Why does it seem like most anything can be done in one minute? Maybe that's just how the universe is constructed. It's probably a good idea because that's about all the time we have to devote to anything. There's even a One Minute Manager and a One Minute Sales Person.

The politician's sudden and unexpected tragedy also has caused me to study the profound questions: "What is really important in life? I mean *really*. What are the world's greatest truths?" And in addition, "How long does it take to learn them: days, weeks, months, maybe years?"

Well, after years of study I finally discovered the truths. But after I spent all that time I was shocked to discover that each can be learned in about 60 seconds or less! It may sound hard to believe, but it's a fact, and I'll prove it to you. Real truth is simple; it's people who complicate things. I wish I had known all this before. But you can. My loss is your gain.

For this reason, I have developed a modern packaging of these ancient truths, and designed them specifically for the modern man or woman, the 20th-century person on the move and who is always in a hurry. If you are really busy but, unlike the poor politician, you are willing to devote at least one minute to something truly important, this book is for you.

Yes, for you—rushed, hurried, harried, anxious, yet worried about "the meaning of life," and the future—I excitedly present:

The World's Greatest Truths...

and I unflinchingly include this claim and guarantee: this book will show you how you can, *in just one minute*, do something that will give you instant and permanent *approval* by the Creator of the universe! Incredible? But true. If you follow the One Minute Procedure later in this book, you can be assured of God's special blessings for all eternity. Otherwise, you can obtain a refund of the full purchase price of this book (if returned in good condition).

Don't scoff. I'm serious. You will be pleasantly surprised at what you discover in the following pages. You will probably never be the same.

There is one secret that makes all this possible. I can't take any credit for it. It's been around for thousands of years. It's really nothing new. But I will tell you what it is. It is, without a doubt, "the world's greatest secret." Surprisingly, this secret has affected millions and millions of people. It has affected the course of empires, and it has changed history.

I will also tell you how this secret and actually all the truths in this book are based on "the world's greatest substance," and how this miraculous substance is the mysterious link between Judaism and Christianity. Someday both Jews and Christians will see and marvel over this link together.

Why such a big secret, and how do I know about it? Well, the only reason it may be a secret now is that truth often becomes obscured over time and by tradition. Sometimes we humans put layers and layers of our own ideas upon basic truths until they are unrecognizable. That's what has happened. But *The World's Greatest Truths* goes to the *original source* to bring you the undiluted, untampered *truth*!

These truths are so simple and wonderful, it's almost too good to be true. But it is. Actually, millions of people constantly refer to them as "amazing."[2]

They really are amazing, and true. I will bet my life on it.

"Can you spare just one minute?"

CHAPTER ONE

The World's Greatest Book

Chapter 1: The World's Greatest Book

It is the best seller of all time, of all books anywhere. It is referred to as "the Book of books." It has been translated into more languages than any book in the world—at least parts of it into over 1,800 languages! It is even believed to be the first book ever translated, from Hebrew to Greek.

We call the book, simply, the Bible. The word Bible means "books." Actually, the Bible is a collection of books—66 of them, written by some 40 authors.

Every valid belief must have a factual basis. There are millions of opinions on almost any subject, but they are only uninformed and meaningless unless they are rooted in fact. The Bible is the root source of the faith of the plurality of the world's population. This raises a major question...

Is the Bible trustworthy? This may be "the world's greatest question." Is it a factual revelation of the Creator of the universe, or just a collection of human opinions and myths? Are there objective reasons why millions of people, including scholars, believe in the Bible's reliability, or is it just a matter of blind faith? You need to know. The entire validity of Judaism, which is based on the Old Testament, and Christianity, which is based on both the Old and New Testaments, rests upon the answer.

If it is not trustworthy, it is the greatest hoax ever fostered upon the human race, and deserves our total scorn. If it is trustworthy, it demands our utmost attention and respect. Only one attitude is incomprehensible—indifference, to strangely ignore the possibility that the Bible may contain the exclusive answers to this life and the next, as it claims. Interestingly, most people, even the indifferent, have an opinion on the subject, although it is often based on emotion or hearsay. But surprisingly few have systematically examined the evidence, or even read it.

I once asked myself this question, and then spent the next 25 years discovering the answer. I'll tell my conclusion, then in just one minute I will summarize the extensive research generally agreed upon by thousands of scholars. Is the Bible trustworthy? You will find out.

Chapter 1: The World's Greatest Book

The Bible Is Unique

Scholars who have studied the sacred writings of the various religions report that the Bible is unique and distinctive for many reasons. Here are a few:

- ☐ It was written over a period of about 1,600 years, or about 40 generations.
- ☐ It was written in different places on three different continents: Asia, Africa, and Europe.
- ☐ It was written in three languages: Hebrew, Aramaic, and Greek.
- ☐ Its 40 authors were from different walks of life, including kings, fishermen, scholars, statesmen, and peasants.
- ☐ It includes hundreds of subjects.

Yet with the above incredible diversity, it has an amazing unity. This continuity and consistency (along with other characteristics and content as described below) make the Bible logically beyond human ability to accomplish. *The presence and influence of an external Guiding Hand are necessary.*

Another unique and undoubtedly miraculous feature is the Bible's *survivability*. It has withstood attacks not given to any other book, attacks from despots, doubters, and skeptics throughout the ages and around the world. Despots hate the freedom it gives to the human spirit and the worship it reserves for God instead of the state or its leader. From the days of the Roman emperors to present-day fascists and communists, the Bible has been outlawed and attempts have been made to stamp it out. Over 200 years ago, Voltaire predicted the Bible's soon demise. Ironically, after his death the Geneva Bible Society used Voltaire's printing press to publish more Bibles. "God is not mocked,"[1] the Bible says.

Doubters are often motivated by the Bible's moral imperatives. One popular modern-day intellectual admitted the Bible's truth but then said he was forced to reject it because to accept it would condemn his "lifestyle." Human pride causes much opposition. The idea is abhorrent to many that their moral condition would cause the need for mercy from the Supreme Being, a need of every human, according to the Bible. They see their outwardly ethical behavior as qualifying them for favor from Almighty God, in a sense making them His moral equal, or Him their debtor.

Intellectual pride is also a factor as doubt has become institutionalized, pervading many universities, including seminaries. Peer pressure forces almost blind faith in the flimsy hypotheses of "higher criticism" to try to prove the Bible writers as either ignorant or liars. Upon receiving solid evidence that a popular such theory was in error, one professor agreed but said he had been teaching it too long to change!

In spite of these unparalleled attacks to destroy it, the Bible has survived as the most authentic and accurate ancient document in existence, based on both age and number of original manuscripts available. Homer's *Iliad* ranks closest to the New Testament in number of manuscripts available, *643*, with the earliest copy written about *500* years after the original. There are only about *10* good manuscripts of Caesar's *Gallic Wars* available and the earliest was written over *900* years after the original. By contrast, there are over 5,000 complete or partial Greek manuscripts of the New Testament available (plus over 10,000 Latin Vulgate and over 9,000 other versions), with the earliest written only *25* years after the original!

Shakespeare's 37 plays are only about 200 years old but there are said to be about 100 significant textual variants that are a subject of scholarly dispute. The New Testament is about 1,900 years old and it is estimated that there are only 20 or less such passages. Do we ever doubt the reliability of Shakespeare's work?

If the same tests were applied to all available ancient literature, the Bible would clearly be hailed as by far the most reliable. Or else all other ancient literature, including the classics, would have to be rejected as unreliable.

Chapter 1: The World's Greatest Book

The Bible Claims Itself To Be Divinely Inspired

A major and unique aspect of the Bible is its own consistent claim to be divinely inspired. The Bible claims itself to be "the Word of God." But more than claiming divine inspiration, in the Bible God even speaks in the first person! Expressions such as "And God said..." followed by a quote appear about 3,800 times in the Old Testament alone.

These claims and characteristics are in a book which espouses truth, morality, and all that is good. It is illogical that it would be a hoax, and a conspiracy is impossible because of the vast differences in time and place of the writers and events. Also, of the large number of people involved, someone would have surely "squealed," a victim of the good conscience he preached. But beyond logic, there are other objective reasons that argue for the divine inspiration of the Bible.

Prophecy Confirms The Bible's Truth

Prophecy, or the prediction of future events, gives the Bible an internal authenticity. This is one of the great marvels of the Bible, one that distinguishes it from all other writings. Prophets spoke under the inspiration of the Holy Spirit about future events, especially concerning Israel, the nations, the Messiah, and the church. The events have occurred without fail as they were predicted. Unlike modern-day psychics whose track record on predictions is, at best, usually no more than chance would provide, the ancient Hebrew prophets could not make a mistake. They were 100% accurate, the only such group in the history of the world. This confirms the divine origin of their information. Through them, God revealed His plans, and they wrote it as they were inspired.

For example, about six hundred years before Christ, the prophet Ezekiel predicted details about the destruction of the city of Tyre.[2] Its destruction by Nebuchadnezzar came just a few years later. History has shown the prophecy's amazing details to have happened: Tyre became a "bare rock" where fishermen spread their nets, and the city was never rebuilt. There were many other prophecies and fulfillments concerning various locations and people, such as Sidon, Samaria, Edom, and Nineveh. Many prophecies foretold the historical plight of the Hebrew people, their first dispersion in 586 B.C. and return under Ezra, and their later dispersion and worldwide persecution foretold by Christ that occurred in A.D. 70. It was also foretold that they would someday return to their land from all over the earth. Seeing this, the prophet Isaiah had said:

> *"Who has heard such a thing? . . . Shall a land be born in one day? Shall a nation be brought forth in one moment?"*[3]

Almost 2,000 years after the Jewish dispersion, the United Nations, in an unprecedented action, mandated the reestablishment of the nation of Israel. Born "in one day," May 14, 1948, modern Israel is seen as prophetic fulfillment by many scholars.

Probably the most profound and intriguing prophecies concern the Messiah, which will be discussed in the next chapter.

Archaeology Confirms The Bible's Truth

The relatively new science of archaeology is confirming the utmost accuracy of the Scriptures as previously unknown records and artifacts are uncovered. For centuries, many people doubted certain details of the Bible, such as the existence of certain ancient peoples and places that seemed in conflict with available knowledge. But by faith alone, the devoted would always cling to the Bible's truth because it was "inspired." Now, just in our generation, doubts have been put aside one-by-one by researchers combing and digging over ancient sites.

For example, the Old Testament refers to a city that was built from solid rock. Skeptics would scoff about the reality of this unknown city, but Petra has been discovered and is now a major tourist stop in Jordan. In the New Testament, in Acts 13:7 Luke speaks of a "proconsul" who was the governor of Cyprus. For years many scholars thought that Luke had made a mistake in terminology

Chapter 1: The World's Greatest Book

because the Roman government was thought to have used the title "propraetor" instead. Recently, however, archaeology has determined that Rome did, in fact, use the title mentioned by Luke. The scoffing critics were found to be in error as they have time after time.

Dr. W. A. Criswell points out that about 200 years ago a group of French scholars listed 82 alleged "errors" in the Bible that would eventually destroy Christianity. Since then, however, archaeology and the increased understanding of the ancient languages and cultural contexts have resolved each item.[4]

Christ Himself Confirms The Bible's Truth

The testimony of Jesus Christ Himself confirms the Bible. Even His detractors exalt His saintliness and wisdom, incapable of deception and misrepresentation. Christ believed and taught the infallibility and reliability of the Scriptures, even rebuking those who did not believe! He repeatedly said such things as: "It is written...Search the Scriptures...Have you read?...Scripture cannot be broken." He spoke confidently and unashamedly of Old Testament events and people, such as Noah and the ark, Jonah and the whale, Abraham, and Moses. He also said that *the story of His own life and purpose was prophetically and symbolically woven through all these actual events hundreds of years before.*

Jesus did not teach that just the principles or basic message of the Scriptures were inspired, or even just the words. He spoke of the accuracy of even the "jot" and "tittle," the smallest characters of the Hebrew alphabet.

And it wasn't just in His human life that Jesus believed and taught the infallibility of the Scriptures. He did so even after the resurrection when He rebuked the disciples as "slow of heart to believe *all* that the prophets have spoken!"[5] (Not some, but *all!*)

Of course, in Jesus' day there was no New Testament. There was only what we call the Old Testament, the Jewish Bible. But Jesus knew the New Testament was forthcoming, and He placed His stamp of authority on it *by anticipation* when He told His disciples:

Chapter 1: The World's Greatest Book

"But the Counselor, the Holy Spirit, whom the Father will send in my name, he will teach you all things, and will bring to your remembrance all that I have said to you."[6]

Mathematical Proof Of The Bible's Truth?

Possible mathematical proof of divine inspiration is one of the most intriguing subjects. The field needs much more research and previous research needs recognition. However, beginning at least as early as the 1,800's and through today, mathematically-gifted people have made exhaustive studies in the original Hebrew and Greek languages of the Bible manuscripts. These researchers claim that results prove that the writings had to come from an infinite and omniscient Mind. One person who studied this phenomenon was a Russian immigrant and Harvard graduate, Dr. Ivan Panin, who spent 50 years and accumulated 43,000 pages of notes on the subject before he died in 1942.[7] A recently published work on the subject is *Theomatics,* by Jerry Lucas and Del Washburn.[8]

In both Hebrew and Greek, numbers are not separate characters but are represented by letters of the alphabet. For example, in Greek "alpha" is both the first letter of the alphabet and also the number one. Panin and others have taken the original manuscripts and have assigned the appropriate numerical value to each letter. Then they looked for numerical patterns.

The results they report are mind-boggling—patterns of numbers that could not have been done by humans. Plus, probability theory analysis shows such an elaborate accident as totally impossible. For example, in the first verse of the Bible, Panin found 30 different patterns of the number seven. In English, this verse has ten words, but in the original Hebrew it has only seven. The seven words have exactly 28 (4 X 7) letters. The nouns in the sentence give a combined 777 (111 X 7). The two objects of the verb both have seven letters, and so on. The chance of 30 combinations of seven in a seven word sentence happening accidentally is described as

Chapter 1: The World's Greatest Book

1 in 33,000,000,000,000!

Lucas, a Phi Beta Kappa, and Washburn report similar and numerous examples in the Greek New Testament manuscripts, and their book includes a 79-page chapter on just their statistical and probability methodology to satisfy sincere and serious doubters. They state unequivocally that their study "scientifically proves that God wrote the Bible."

Such patterns as discovered by Panin, Lucas, and Washburn are said to appear throughout both the Old and New Testaments and supposedly *have not been found in any other writing anywhere.*

In a startling announcement carried by the Associated Press, researchers at the Israel Institute of Technology have discovered a similar, but different, phenomenon. Using computer analysis of the first five books of the Bible, or Jewish Torah, they have discovered odd patterns of hidden words with coded intervals. For example, in the book of Genesis, the Hebrew word "Torah" is found repeated by letters at 50-character intervals and "Elohim" (God) at 26-character intervals. The word "holocaust" is reportedly found at 50-character intervals in Deuteronomy, a book that predicts great future trouble for the Israelite people (chapters 28-31). It would have been impossible for a mortal to have done this, and statistically such an accident would have been impossible, the researchers say. "We need a non-rational explanation. And ours is that (it) was written by God through the hand of Moses," says computer expert, Menachem Wiener, of the Institute.[9]

In all of this, it appears that the omniscient Creator left a most unusual and persuasive signature on His Word. It makes the apostle Paul's statement even more graphic and awesome:

"All Scripture is God-breathed..."[10]

Is the Bible trustworthy? We have not even mentioned the reality of its truths that have been experienced by millions of people over the centuries. But the collective evidence that we have included overwhelmingly supports the fact that the Bible is God's unique and, as it claims, exclusive message to the human race. We must not ignore it.[11]

Understanding the Bible

The Bible is a collection of history, biography, poetry, prophecy, and spiritual and practical principles. But there are many things in it that are difficult to understand. Perhaps that is because the Bible is revelation from the infinite Mind. Also, the Bible reveals that God desires "seekers." And when we read it, we are plumbing the depths of the infinite. We should not despair if we do not understand everything. No one does.

The Bible has been described as a deep mine of treasures, continually inviting the seeker to another chamber after he has spent time in the first. In writing to his son in A.D. 412, St. Augustine said:

> *"Such is the depth of the Christian Scriptures that even if I were attempting to study them and nothing else from early boyhood to decrepit old age, with the utmost leisure, the most unwearied zeal, and talents greater than I have, I would still daily be making progress in discovering their treasures."*

Here are some principles that will help you to understand the deeper messages of the Bible. Approach it prayerfully, and know that only God can unlock its mysteries for you. Avoid interpreting passages out of context. Compare difficult passages with passages that are clear and look for consistent truths or themes. Consider the historical context. Finally, use a good modern translation, and a lexicon or commentary to clarify unfamiliar words and concepts.

Words Of Life

In the Bible you will find words of the Spirit, for your spirit.[12] You will find who you are, where you came from, and where you are going. No other book or source anywhere in the world has that information. *You will find yourself* and the meaning of life. You will also discover "the world's greatest person," who we describe in the next chapter. Good reading!

ONE MINUTE SUMMARY
The World's Greatest Book

The Bible is the the most unusual book ever written and the best seller of all time. An array of incontrovertible facts gives overwhelming evidence of the Bible's divine origin and complete trustworthiness: (1) by virtue of the number of copies or parts of ancient manuscripts extant, their closeness in years to the original, and the agreement of scholars on their accuracy, the Bible is by far the most reliable of all ancient works, much more so than the next most reliable, Homer's *Iliad*; (2) it was written over a period of about 1,600 years, on three continents, in three languages, and by some 40 authors ranging from peasants to kings. In spite of that, it has an amazing consistency and continuity, making an external Guiding Hand an obvious necessity; (3) the Bible uniquely claims itself to be divine, and in its pages God speaks even in the first person; (4) prophecy and later exact fulfillment give the Bible an internal authenticity; (5) the modern science of archaeology has consistently confirmed the Bible's most minute details, silencing previous critics and scoffers; (6) Jesus Christ Himself believed and taught the Bible's complete accuracy, both before and after His resurrection, even to the "jot" and "tittle," the smallest components of the Hebrew alphabet; (7) while less conclusive without further research, modern computer and mathematical analysis has revealed evidence of previously hidden word and number patterns that could not have been placed by mortals or occurred by chance—apparently a divine signature of the Creator to further authenticate His work and to demonstrate His power. In conclusion, all objective evidence supports the statement of the apostle Paul who said, "All Scripture is God-breathed."

Chapter 1: The World's Greatest Book

"All Scripture is God-breathed"

CHAPTER **TWO**

The World's Greatest Person

Chapter 2: The World's Greatest Person

Consider the unusual person described in the classic essay, *One Solitary Life*:

"Here was a man who was born in an obscure village, the child of a peasant woman. He grew up in another village. He worked in a carpenter shop until he was thirty, and then for three years he was an itinerant preacher. He never owned a home. He never wrote a book. He never held an office. He never had a family. He never went to college. He never put his feet inside a big city. He never traveled 200 miles from the place where he was born. He never did one of the things that usually accompany greatness. He had no credentials but himself.... While still a young man, the tide of popular opinion turned against him. His friends ran away. One of them denied him. He was turned over to his enemies. He went through the mockery of a trial. He was nailed upon a cross between two thieves. While he was dying, his executioners gambled for the only piece of property he had on earth—his coat. When he was dead, he was taken down and laid in a borrowed grave through the pity of a friend.

"Nineteen long centuries have come and gone and today he is the centerpiece of the human race and the leader of the column of progress. I am far within the mark when I say that all the armies that ever marched, all the navies that ever were built, all the parliaments that ever sat, and all the kings that ever reigned, put together, have not affected the life of man upon this earth as powerfully as that one solitary life."[1]

An Unusual Jew

The above is a fascinating and intriguing description, and a true one. But unfortunately, it leaves out one major point and thus falls far short. The person described was more than just an obscure man who left a major impact on the world. *He actually claimed to be God in human form*!

The person? A Jew named Yeshua, better known in English as Jesus. By virtue of His identity and influence, He is undoubtedly "the world's greatest person." You've probably heard something about Him, but if you are like most people there are probably some startling things you have never been told. You need to know the truth.

An Incredible Claim

God in human form? An incredible claim. Do you believe it? Well, you may be surprised to learn that in a Gallup poll, 42% of the respondents in 20th-century America said that they believed it. And I suspect most of the rest have never really investigated the evidence, which is overwhelming. Consider:

1. Jesus claimed to fulfill all the Hebrew prophecies of the coming Messiah and did.[2] Scholars count hundreds of prophetic passages in the Old Testament (Jewish Bible) that referred to Jesus—His virgin birth, His birthplace, the time of His coming, His miracles, His suffering and resurrection, and many others. What are the "odds" that such prophecies could be fulfilled by "chance" in Jesus or anyone else? One scholar has calculated the odds for just eight prophecies fulfilled in one person as 1 in 10^{17}, or 1 in 100,000,000,000,000,000. For 48 of them, the odds would be 1 in 10^{157}, or 157 zeros! In other words, it would be virtually impossible.

2. He claimed to be the same one who had revealed Himself to Moses in Egypt centuries before.[3]

3. He claimed to be the bodily form of God the Father.[4]

4. He claimed to forgive sins.[5]

5. He reinterpreted and clarified the Ten Commandments, revealing the intent or "spirit" of the law and not just the letter of it.[6]

6. He predicted His death and resurrection.[7]

7. He received and accepted worship through the titles of "Lord," and "God."[8]

8. He predicted a second, and next time majestic visitation to the earth at an undesignated time in the future to usher in a new era.[9]

9. He claimed to be the final judge of the whole world and each person in it.[10]

10. He claimed the authority to grant a never-ending existence in a paradise-like environment to those who recognize His identity and put their trust in Him.[11]

11. Whether one likes it or not, He unmistakably claimed exclusivity—that He is the only way (a concept made understandable by Chapters 4, 5, and 6 of this book).[12]

12. He backed his words with displays of power over nature never seen on the earth, before or since.[13]

13. As He predicted, three days after His execution He was resurrected, of which we have many eyewitness accounts. He was reportedly seen by more than 500 people.[14]

14. All the above is documented in what is considered the most amazingly preserved and reliable ancient document in existence (see Chapter 1). Also, this real and dynamic truth has been experienced in millions, probably billions, of lives over almost 2,000 years.

Just A Great Moral Teacher?

Satisfied? Or do you still think that perhaps Jesus was just a good man, or a great teacher, or maybe just one of many prophets? Some who are not aware of His claims, or the evidence, or who have not thought it through may think that. But such an idea is logically insupportable, according to the late Cambridge University professor and British author, C.S. Lewis, who incisively concluded:

> *"A man who was merely a man and said the sort of things that Jesus said would not be a great moral teacher. He would either be a lunatic—on a level with a man who says he is a poached egg—or else he would be the Devil*

of Hell. You must make your choice. Either this man was, and is, the Son of God: or else a madman or something worse. You can shut him up for a fool, you can spit on him and kill him as a demon; or you can fall at his feet and call him Lord and God. But let us not come with any patronizing nonsense about his being a great human teacher. He has not left that open to us. He did not intend to."[15]

To paraphrase Lewis: considering the things that Jesus said about Himself, He would have to be a complete *liar*, a hopeless *lunatic*, or the *Lord*. There is no rational basis for the first two.

Napoleon Bonaparte's words summarize a prevailing view of Jesus:

"I know men and I tell you that Jesus Christ is no mere man. Between him and every other person in the world is no possible term of comparison."[16]

While truth does not always win the popularity contest and is really not dependent upon a vote, it is significant that in the world today there are more people who claim Christianity than any other religion. According to some studies, their numbers are equivalent to the next two largest combined, Islam and Hinduism, but statistics in this area are at best estimates. Also, in many cultures religious faith is identified with nationality and not with personal belief and commitment. (In most Christianized cultures, however, there is relative freedom of religion and expression; other religious cultures are often closed and repressive toward other beliefs.)

Critical Distinctions

There are great distinctions between Yeshua, or Jesus, and all others who are considered "religious founders." The 14 points above cover many of them. Four which stand out are:

Jesus' life was predicted in advance, and in considerable detail. This amazing fact authenticated His identity and claims. This has happened to no other person, ever.

Jesus claimed to be God. Few others ever made such a claim. Most were not even trying to start a "new religion." Hinduism did not even have a founder, but evolved from local practices and foreign invaders. Some say that Hinduism is not even a religion and impossible to define because it stands for everything and thus for nothing. Japan's Shintoism, which saw the Emperor Hirohito as God, was discredited when Japan lost World War II, causing Hirohito to disavow his deity.

Jesus claimed to be "the Way." The others generally tried to describe what they thought was *a way*. Lao Tzu (Taoism) recognized an ultimate truth but admitted he could not define it (but strangely referred to it as a "Son"). K'ung Fu-tzu (Confucious) never really intended to start a religion but only to outline an ethical system. Buddhism is primarily an ethical system. Its founder, Siddhartha Gautama, like the others, never claimed to be divine or even to have divine revelation. But overzealous followers later deified him. Jesus summarized all valid ethics in just one word—love, a concept He was sent to personify. He also said, "No one comes to the Father but by me."[17]

Jesus was resurrected, leaving an empty grave. The others, like all humans, died and remained dead. Even though Gautama died about four centuries before Jesus was born, parts of his body, such as hair and teeth, are still preserved and enshrined. (See Appendix I for a further discussion of world religions.)

Historical Impact

Jesus came and "punctuated" human history, dividing it between B.C. (before Christ) and A.D. (anno Domini—"in the year of our Lord"). Our calendars are dated by His incarnation ("incarnate"—in human form). Every letter, newspaper, magazine and, in fact, nearly every document honors Him by showing the years since He was on the earth.

History is *His*-story. Have you ever wondered if human history has any purpose, if there is any rhyme or reason to the rise and fall of nations and empires or for the vicissitudes of human activity?

Chapter 2: The World's Greatest Person

Atheistic materialism would tell us that we're here as a result of cosmic accident, that we evolved from the chance collision of sea slime molecules, and that we're going nowhere. Even if humanity progresses, someday it will all be wiped out when the sun burns out and the solar system becomes extinct. Ultimately, according to this view, life is a giant mistake, and all that we hold dear is a cruel joke. But the Bible tells us that God does indeed have a *plan* for history:

> *"For God has allowed us to know the secret of his plan, and it is this: he purposes in his sovereign will that all human history be consummated in Christ, that everything that exists in Heaven or earth shall find its perfection and fulfillment in him."*[18]

The influence of Christ on our own civilization has been foundational and pervasive. The famous British historian, Arnold Toynbee, described Christianity as the "chrysalis" from which the entire Western civilization emerged.[19]

Although he was not the first human in the New World, Christopher Columbus started the chain of events in the 1400's that led to our present society. His first name actually means "Christ-bearer," and his last name "dove," the symbol of the Holy Spirit. Columbus was a devout believer in Christ, and he was convinced that God had given him a divine mission: to carry the light of Christ to undiscovered lands.[20] At his first stop upon reaching the New World, Columbus gave it a very special name: San Salvador, meaning "Holy Savior." He planted a cross everywhere he landed and dedicated the place to God.

Later, the first permanent English-speaking settlement in the New World at Jamestown in 1607 had as its "principal and main ends....to preach....and the propagation of the gospel..."[21] A few years afterward, in 1620, the settlers at Plymouth expressed a similar motivation in the Mayflower Compact.

A biblical world view undergirds the framing documents of our nation. Recent research has shown that all but a very few of the men who wrote the United States Constitution were orthodox in their Christian faith and not deists as some cynically claim. Thomas Jefferson and Benjamin Franklin, while not known as orthodox Christians, are claimed by some to have been deists. However, we know that they had biblically-influenced views of life and human nature and made statements incompatible with deism (deism recognizes a God but sees Him as an absentee landlord who never interferes with the world or humanity, meaning the Bible cannot be inspired, prayer is futile, and Jesus cannot be divine). Historian C. Gregg Singer states that at the constitutional convention, "It is conceded that a more Christian philosophy permeated the thinking and actions of the members."[22] They derived much of their thought from authors such as John Locke and William Blackstone who got most of their ideas from the Bible.

Even the concepts of private property and free enterprise have biblical roots. Both the Jamestown and Plymouth settlements initially attempted a collectivism (communism) type of economic arrangement but it proved disastrously inefficient and of short duration. For example, at Plymouth, a new Governor Bradford wisely switched to private farming. Production dramatically increased and famine ceased. Bradford criticized the former leadership for denying private property and the attempt at a communistic economy, chiding, "as if they were wiser than God."[23]

Perhaps John Quincy Adams said it best:

"The highest glory of the American Revolution was this: it connected in one indissoluble bond, the principles of civil government and the principles of Christianity."[23]

One may wonder about the following constitutional provision: "The church....shall be separated from the state and the school from the church." However, most are surprised to learn that the phrase is from Article 53 of the Constitution of the *USSR*. The U. S. Constitution prohibits any law respecting the establishment of religion, or *prohibiting the free exercise thereof*. It does not mention separation of church and state. This basically means that government cannot establish or interfere with religion. It does not prevent religious conviction from affecting the process of

43

Chapter 2: The World's Greatest Person

government. For example, most criminal laws (murder, theft, etc.) reflect the standards of Judeo-Christian heritage. Laws always have their roots in the mores of a culture, and mores spring from a people's view of life and reality.

The influence of Christ also pervaded the nation's early institutions. For example, history has largely ignored the fact that fully 104 of the first 119 colleges founded in the United States were Christian and dedicated to the idea that God is the basis of all knowledge. Harvard had in its laws that each student should consider: "The main end of his life and studies to know God and Jesus Christ....and therefore to lay Christ....as the only foundation for all sound learning and knowledge." Yale, Columbia, and Princeton had similar roots.

In spite of the shortcomings of our nation and our people (and there are many), people all over the world recognize that the concept and the dynamic of the free human spirit and the historic values represented in America, which sprang from its Christian roots, are the only things preventing the entire world from being swallowed into the dark spiritual abyss of atheistic, materialistic, and totalitarian communism. Sadly and alarmingly, there are those even in our own nation who are bent on destroying these roots and who would lead us toward cultural suicide. It makes the words of Dr. Jedediah Morse in 1799, close to 200 years ago, both relevant and prophetic:

> *"To the kindly influence of Christianity we owe that degree of civil freedom, and political and social happiness which mankind now enjoys. In proportion as the genuine effects of Christianity are diminished in any nation, either through unbelief, or the corruption of its doctrines, or the neglect of its institutions; in the same proportion will the people of that nation recede from the blessings of genuine freedom.... Whenever the pillars of Christianity shall be over thrown, our present republican forms of government, and all the blessings which flow from them, must fall with them."*[24]

Chapter 2: The World's Greatest Person

Morse's observation is not a pious platitude but is based on a psychological fact. Commitment to Christ and His rule in one's personal life brings self-restraint in human relationships. A person must be ruled from within or from without, either through restraining self or being restrained. Lack of self-restraint always results in either anarchy or repression. In 1852, Robert C. Winthrop made an interesting comment on this principle:

> *"All societies must be governed in some way or other. The less they may have of stringent state government, the more they must have of individual self-government. The less they rely on public law or physical force, the more they must rely on private moral restraint.*
>
> *"Men, in a word, must necessarily be controlled, either by a power within them, or by a power without them; either by the Word of God, or by the strong arm of man; either by the Bible, or by the bayonet."*[25]

The global effects in this century of that "one solitary life" are subtle, often unrecognized, but nevertheless pervasive. They touch in one way or another most, if not all, of the earth's billions of inhabitants.

Rather than further examining the effect of Jesus upon temporal nations and institutions, it is more important to discover His effect upon individual people, each of whom is a priceless and eternal entity. For these individuals the life of Jesus unlocked and explained a "secret" which had been hidden ever since the world was created. It is really "the world's greatest secret," and it is the subject of the next chapter.

00:01:00

ONE MINUTE SUMMARY
The World's Greatest Person

Poverty, no college degree, little travel, no public office, and executed as a common criminal while still young—yet almost 2,000 years later He has had more of an impact on the empires, institutions, and the people of the earth than any person who has ever lived—a Jew named Yeshua, or Jesus, whose visit to the earth was described before He was born in great detail by the ancient Hebrew prophets.

He claimed to be *God in human form*. His claim was substantiated by the fulfillment of all the prophecies of the coming Messiah, by the supernatural power He displayed, by the divine authority by which He spoke, and by His resurrection from the dead witnessed by many. His claims about Himself would logically rule Him out as just a "good moral teacher" or great prophet. He would have to be (1) a complete *liar*, (2) a hopeless *lunatic*, or (3) the *Lord*, and there is no rational basis for the first two.

Jesus is distinctively different from all others who are considered to be religious "founders." He claimed to be God, and His life, actions, and words proved it. The others never made such a claim and in most cases never even claimed divine revelation. Jesus claimed to be "the Way." The others suggested "a way," primarily of ethical living. He personified the summation of all valid ethics—love. He was resurrected, leaving an empty grave. The others died as humans, and remained dead. Jesus punctuated human history, and the influence of His life soon permeated the Roman empire, setting the course for future civilizations, their institutions, and billions of lives yet unborn.

CHAPTER THREE

The World's Greatest Secret

Chapter 3: The World's Greatest Secret

This book is for people who like to get to the point in a hurry. Actually, I was going to give you the background and explanation first, then save the big *secret* until the very last chapter. But it's so great I just can't wait. I've got to give it to you now. You can't do anything in one minute and waste any time. Besides, I'm not one to beat around the bush, probably the reason I'm writing this unusual book. I'm in a hurry. Aren't you? So here it is.

The person who wrote the most about this secret and, in fact, who wrote most of the New Testament, was a man on the move. He also must have been in a hurry most of the time, as evidenced by his tremendous accomplishments. His name was Paul. He was of the tribe of Benjamin, and a Pharisee—a "Hebrew of Hebrews" he called himself—the consummate Jew. He was a scholar, having received strict schooling on Jewish law and tradition from Gamaliel, one of the great Judaic teachers of the day.

This is an important point: Paul (formerly called Saul) was intimately aware of the revelations of the Jewish Scriptures, or Jewish Bible—what Christians call the Old Testament today. No one was going to fool him or involve him with any kind of new religion or sect. In fact, he was so zealous for and protective of traditional Judaism that he became one of the leading persecutors of those who believed that another Jew, Yeshua (Jesus), had fulfilled the ancient Hebrew prophecies of the coming Messiah and had risen from the dead. The number of these Jewish believers had risen into many thousands and was growing daily. Paul furiously opposed them, and even assented to their deaths.

A Supernatural Encounter

But one day while on his way to Damascus to take some of these believers captive, he had a dramatic, supernatural encounter with this resurrected Jesus. In a blinding light and with a voice from heaven, Jesus revealed Himself to Paul. It was so real that

Chapter 3: The World's Greatest Secret

Paul's life was instantly and totally changed. He now knew experientially that Jesus was indeed alive. In an instant reversal of his whole life's direction, Paul called Him "Lord" and purposed to obey His instructions. This was probably the most dramatic and instant change of any person in history.

Scholar that he was, Paul then studied the ancient Scriptures intensely and saw that Yeshua had, in fact, fulfilled the messianic prophecies. With his training in Judaism coupled to his actual encounter with the risen Messiah plus later study, this Jew, Paul, probably had a deeper comprehension of the spiritual truth that embraced both centuries-old Judaism and the new messianic faith (later called Christianity) than any person who has ever lived. It is no accident that Paul was chosen by Jesus to take His message to the Roman empire and to write most of the New Testament. This message soon permeated the empire and largely laid the foundation for future civilization and institutions as we know them. Paul had discovered the *secret*.

A Mystery Unveiled

Years after his life-changing experience and later study, Paul wrote about a mystery

"which was kept secret for long ages but is now disclosed and through the prophetic writings is made known to all nations."[1]

Another Jew, Peter, told us that the ancient Hebrew prophets searched and inquired about this secret but didn't understand it, and that even angels longed to see it but apparently could not.[2] You are about to see what angels had not been able to see, and what the Hebrew prophets wrote about but really didn't understand!

For example, about 700 B.C., the Hebrew prophet, Isaiah, wrote about a great Person who was to be born at some future time. Here are some of the things he said:

Chapter 3: The World's Greatest Secret

> *"The Lord himself shall give you a sign; Behold, a <u>virgin</u> shall conceive, and bare a <u>son</u>, and shall call his name Immanuel (which means 'God with us').*[3]
> *"Unto us a <u>son</u> is given....and his name shall be called.... The mighty God, The everlasting Father, the Prince of Peace.*[4]
> *"He is despised and rejected of men....he was wounded for our transgressions, he was bruised for our iniquities....he is brought as a <u>lamb</u> to the slaughter....thou shalt make his soul an offering for sin."*[5]

Isaiah detailed these facts *seven centuries before Christ was born*! (Clarification: there is a weak argument that the Hebrew word, *almah*, for "virgin" above doesn't necessarily mean virgin. It can mean just a "maiden"; however, the context here proves its translation as "virgin"—that it was a God-given "sign." A normal birth obviously would not be a sign. Also, the New Testament Greek accounts confirm the meaning. Further, a God/human conception was necessary for the incarnation, a concept made understandable by Chapters 4, 5, and 6 of this book.)

Scholars refer to a "messianic thread" running throughout the entire Old Testament that refers to a coming Savior and Deliverer. Bible-believing Jews still look for Him and know that He will come some day. But even though Jesus was a Jew, all His disciples were Jews, most of His early followers were Jews, and by the end of the first century an estimated one million Jews in the world (in a relatively small world population) believed that Yeshua was the Messiah, many still do not believe.

With all the prophetic confirmations, their disbelief has always been a curiosity. But a study of the Hebrew prophets shows many references to *two* appearances of the Messiah on the earth: the first appearance, as Isaiah mentioned above, was to be in humility—in a human frame, of a human mother, as a servant, to suffer for "our transgressions"; the second and later appearance is to be in power and majesty, to usher in a new era of history.

51

Chapter 3: The World's Greatest Secret

Jesus was the only person in history ever preannounced. Even the Gentile world was looking for the coming Messiah. Tacitus records that in Rome people were persuaded that the "Master" of the world was coming from Judea. Suetonius reiterated that idea. The Greeks also expected Him; Aeschylus spoke of God appearing on earth "to accept upon His head the pangs of thy own sins vicarious." The Fourth Eclogue of Virgil spoke of "a chaste woman, smiling on her infant boy, with whom the iron age would pass away." There is other evidence, even in Chinese history.[6]

When Jesus was on the earth and in the decades following, many, many Jews recognized His identity. But others—those with a political agenda—wanted a Messiah to deliver the nation from Roman rule and to bring them power. And the religious leaders whom Jesus rebuked and called "hypocrites" wanted no part of Him. Jesus spoke of the *spirit* of the law of God, love and servitude, whereas they enjoyed the authority and prestige of enforcing the *letter* of the law on others. Their hearts blinded them from understanding that Messiah's first appearance on earth was to establish a spiritual kingdom, not a political one, which would come later.

Many Jews today believe that Yeshua was the prophesied Messiah but, of course, many do not. This is a great spiritual mystery and is discussed by Paul in the eleventh chapter of the Book of Romans. A contributing factor today is surely the evil persecution that has been inflicted upon the Jewish people by misguided Gentiles in the name of Christianity, a tragedy of history. But oddly, Judaism to a great many Jews is primarily a cultural and ethnic identification rather than a religion based on faith and practice, with even their own Scriptures or history not seen as divinely influenced. In fairness, however, many people also name Christianity as their affiliation with no apparent faith, commitment, or attempt to follow and obey Christ.

But the prophecies were very specific and unmistakable—a virgin mother, a son called "God with us" and "Prince of Peace," a *lamb* who was slaughtered, born in Bethlehem, and scores of others. The prophet Daniel even predicted the time of His coming. One person in history, and only one, has come on the scene and met *all* the criteria.

When Jesus first made his public appearance, the Hebrew prophet, John, saw Him and said, "Behold, the Lamb of God."[7] John knew from the prophecies that Messiah was coming, and coming as a sacrificial "lamb." He recognized Jesus when they encountered at the Jordan River. John confirms the title "lamb" at the very beginning of Jesus' ministry before there was any hint of the possibility of His later execution. John understood the prophecies.

During His three years of public ministry, Jesus unlocked many spiritual mysteries. He clarified the divine law, taught about love, and gave guidelines on how to receive eternal life with God. And finally, just as Isaiah had prophesied, He "was led like a lamb to the slaughter," and was executed as a common criminal, suffering probably the most tortuous execution ever devised by man—a Roman crucifixion.

The Secret

So, what is the *secret*?

Strangely, almost 2,000 years later, it is hard to view a sporting event on television without seeing reference to the *secret*. I have seen it during just about every Super Bowl. The other day, with probably millions of other viewers, I was watching a game and saw it! Behind the announcer on the field, someone purposely stepped in front of the camera's view and held up a sign for the entire national TV audience to see. The sign read simply:

"John 3:16"

There are many ways in which the *secret* could be described, but probably no way of stating it is more clear, more profound, more simple and to the point, and more universally known than John 3:16—the sixteenth verse of the third chapter of the Gospel of John in the New Testament:

> *"For God so loved the world, that he gave his only Son, that whoever believes in him should not perish but have eternal life"*[8]

Chapter 3: The World's Greatest Secret

These are the words of Jesus, Himself, recorded by another John, the disciple. Just 24 words. You can read them out loud comfortably in just *seven seconds*. In less than one minute, just seven seconds, you can absorb them into your spirit. They become a part of your being.

This is the *secret*. Read it again. Look at the key words—God....loved....world....gave....Son....believes....life.

You can easily understand the idea of *God*. You can also easily understand that God can *love*. I'll assume you can grasp that. But what I want to explain now is the aspect where, in order to express this love, God *gave* His *Son*. And I will explain the rationale of how "believing" this can give you "eternal life."

Now it's explanation time. You've learned the secret. But why and how does it work? The mystery and explanation of this secret lie in "the world's greatest substance," the subject of the next chapter.

00:01:00

ONE MINUTE SUMMARY
The World's Greatest Secret

There was a mystery, a secret, that was hidden throughout human history. But hints of it were given and predictions were made through God's prophets. Although the Hebrew prophets wrote as they were inspired, they really didn't understand their own writings. They knew that God was unfolding a wonderful plan but they could not grasp its full significance. It was a spiritual truth hidden even from the angels.

The prophets wrote about a *son* to come, who would be born of a *virgin*, and who would be called "the mighty God," "the Prince of Peace," and "God with us." They gave the place where He would be born, Bethlehem, and the actual timing of His arrival. They wrote that He would be slaughtered as a sacrificial lamb as an offering for sin. There were scores of other prophecies and prophetic symbolisms of a coming and great Person and sacrifice.

The secret was unveiled. All the messianic prophecies were fulfilled in a Jew named Yeshua, or Jesus. When the prophet John first saw Him, he exclaimed, "Behold, the Lamb of God." Jesus did become a sacrificial lamb, died and was raised from the dead. After the resurrection, He appeared to many and later to Paul, a Jew and Hebrew scholar, dramatically changing his life. Paul and the other apostles carried the revealed secret to the world, affecting the course of empires and history. The *secret* is:

"For God so loved the world that he gave his only Son, that whoever believes in him should not perish but have eternal life."

CHAPTER FOUR

The World's Greatest Substance

Chapter 4: The World's Greatest Substance

In all the world, there is only one substance that truly represents life. Ironically, this same substance is also thought of as representing death. Actually, the substance itself contains and sustains life, and the absence or loss of it is usually associated with death. It is a miraculous substance.

Strangely, however, in spite of is marvelous and miraculous nature and unlike any other substance, just the sight of it often makes people sick! Some even faint. Just seeing it traumatizes some people. And even though the substance gives life, when life ends this same substance can create a frightful and messy scene. It can cause a sickening sight.

Also, strangely, scientific statements were made about this substance in the writings of the Bible thousands of years before science as we know it really existed. From Genesis, the first book, to Revelation, the last, the wonderful substance is mentioned in what some call a "scarlet thread" that runs throughout the entire Bible.

The substance is liquid. The substance is red. The substance is...

BLOOD!

Some say that Christianity is a "bloody" religion because of its emphasis on Jesus' blood, a mystery which will be explained in this chapter. Actually Judaism, which gave birth to Christianity, is even bloodier. Today blood sacrifices are no longer offered, but for centuries animal sacrifice was a common practice in Judaism. The Jewish-Roman historian, Josephus, records that there were 255,600 animals slaughtered in Jerusalem at one Jewish Passover observance in the first century.[1] Blood from the altar actually ran in the streets. But there is a critically important reason why blood is foundational to both Judaism and Christianity—*the symbolism seen in the former foreshadowed the reality to come in the latter*!

Chapter 4: The World's Greatest Substance

The latter finally gave needed meaning to the former; without the meaning, the rituals would have been nonsensical and are probably considered such by those who do not understand.

The Passover was an annual event. If approximately that many lambs were slain each year, think how many died over the centuries from this practice. Yet, *each little lamb was symbolic and prophetic of a human Lamb,* the coming Messiah, about whom the prophet Isaiah had said, "He was led like a *lamb* to the slaughter." Just think, for centuries the Israelites were obedient to God in their blood sacrifice rituals, not having any idea of their symbolism or their real and ultimate purpose (a lesson for us to be obedient even though we may not understand everything). But blood sacrifice didn't start with the Israelites; it is traced to the beginning of human history.

The reverence for blood seems universal throughout all cultures. Anthropologists find widespread practices of blood sacrifice to idols from earliest human history and even through today, and also the use of blood as a means of ratifying an agreement, or "covenant," between people.[2] There is an innate human awareness, put there by God Himself, of the solemn importance and spiritual ramifications of blood. But only hints of truth, combined with superstition and paganism, produce perversions of belief and practice as exist in some of the world today. Without full revelation, the peoples of the world have seen only shadows of spiritual truth. And with the spiritual significance of blood, as with other spiritual truths, God used the Hebrew people to most clearly communicate and implement His plan and purpose.

"The Jews are entrusted with the oracles of God."[3]

Life Is In The Blood

Medical science now knows it is blood that transports oxygen and other nutrients throughout the entire body via an ingenious 60,000 mile circulatory network. Vessels ranging from major arteries down to capillaries measuring one-tenth the diameter of a human hair carry life to each of the approximately one hundred trillion cells in our bodies. The food is carried along in this stream of liquid by blood cells, like containers sloshing through a gigantic pipeline. There may be five million or more red blood cells in just one drop of blood. Upon this continuous, moment by moment, supply of food, our entire body depends for life itself. For example, our brain will remain alive only for about five minutes without it. The blood carries life to our whole body.

What is equally amazing, however, is that some 3,500 years ago and before modern medical knowledge, the Lord said to Moses:

"The life of the flesh is in the blood."[4]

The scientific accuracy of the statement at that time in history confirms its divine origin. Moses had no way of knowing of its truth.

But blood sustains life in another way besides transporting food and oxygen. After the blood delivers its cargo, it picks up waste material to transport on the return trip! It not only nourishes but cleanses every cell in the human body, removing toxic material that, if not removed, would otherwise quickly accumulate and kill us. The blood literally *washes* each cell, then carries the waste material away for filtering and disposal.

Again, it is equally amazing that almost 2,000 years ago the apostle John wrote that the Messiah

"washed us from our sins in his own blood."[5]

In those days blood was logically looked upon as something that soiled and stained. Other than from divine inspiration, there was no rational basis for attributing such a "cleansing" function to blood. John also wrote:

"The blood of Jesus his Son cleanses us from all sin."[6]

This gives a totally new perspective to sin and its consequence. Bodily poisons and waste can bring physical death unless continually "washed" away by the blood. Similarly, sin can bring spiritual death

Chapter 4: The World's Greatest Substance

unless continually "washed" away by the blood. And like human blood in our human bodies, in a mystical sense the blood of Messiah is continually washing and cleansing His spiritual body. In another fascinating anatomical comparison, believers in Christ are referred to in the Bible as the "body" of Christ, with Christ the head and everyone else as members. The blood of Christ is continually supplying *life* to His body, and simultaneously *cleansing* from impurities—the very functions of actual blood. And all this was written almost 2,000 years ago before science really knew anything of bodily functions!

World-renowned surgeon, Dr. Paul Brand and Philip Yancey skillfully describe the medical marvels of the human body and its metaphorical counterpart, the spiritual body, in their book, *In His Image*.[7] I highly recommend this fascinating volume.

The Eternal Blood Covenant

The basic functions of Messiah's blood are not an isolated concept in the Old and New Testaments but are a constant theme, a theme which, in fact, is too little known, understood, or appreciated. This chapter and its One Minute Summary will describe this deeply mystical yet practical truth—*the eternal blood covenant.* It is probably the most profound truth in the universe and in all of the history of the human race.

A "covenant" is a *binding* pledge, promise, or agreement between two parties (the words "covenant" and "testament" are synonyms; the two parts of the Bible are sometimes called the Old Covenant and the New Covenant).

"Cutting a covenant" was an ancient practice, not just with the Hebrews but also in other nations and cultures. It involved the cutting of flesh (animal or human) and the shedding of blood to seal this binding agreement. A blood covenant was the most sacred and solemn of contracts, even bringing an inter-union of the two parties (see Chapter 8 for elaboration of the inter-union concept). *It was a completely unbreakable pledge,* not revokable for any reason (this in itself has profound theological implications). Foreshadowing the eternal blood covenant to come, God made a covenant with Abraham:

> *"I will make my covenant between me and you, and will multiply you exceedingly."*[8]

Abraham's part of the covenant was to institute the rite of circumcision, as "a sign of the covenant."[9] Circumcision, of course, "cuts" flesh and sheds blood, a bloodletting/covenant act which foreshadowed the time when God would also shed His own blood in a covenant act. (But why on such an odd and humbling part of the male anatomy? A mystery. But God is never arbitrary. Perhaps it is because in God's perspective it represents the human instrument for the inter-union of beings, from which comes new life, all symbolic.) The story of Abraham contains further symbolism that relates to the New Testament, such as belief in a *miraculous birth* (Isaac), offering his *only son* (by Sarah) as a sacrifice, and belief that his son would be *resurrected*—all pointing to the miraculous birth, death, and resurrection of the Son.

Through the Hebrew prophets God spoke of a "new covenant" to come in the future. It would be for all the people of the world, not just the Hebrew people. The Messiah would be the mediator of this new covenant, and it would be *ratified in His own blood*.[10]

The Last Passover Lamb

At the "last supper" before His crucifixion, Jesus was at the table with His disciples. It is deeply significant that they were eating the traditional Passover meal. Because of the rapid Hellenization of Christianity in the first century as it spread throughout the Gentile world, many forget its totally Jewish origin. Jesus was a strict Hebrew, always observant of the law. The Passover meal itself is rich in tradition and symbolism, its origin tracing to the exodus of the Israelites from Egypt some 1,500 years earlier. God had told those early Israelites to take the blood of an *unblemished male lamb* and put it on their doorposts, then eat the lamb. The blood, He

Chapter 4: The World's Greatest Substance

said, would protect them from death. God said He would "pass over" them when He saw the blood, thus the term *Passover*. And as we shall see, "eating" the lamb had great prophetic significance.

It is ironic but providential that the true Passover Lamb was Himself eating the traditional Passover meal just hours before His own blood would be shed, finally fulfilling centuries of prophecy and symbolism. In fact, the miraculous chronology of events during this time is fascinating. The slaying of Jesus, the true Lamb, coincided with the sacrifice of the other symbolic lambs during this Passover! This in itself is absolutely amazing timing and evidence of the divine plan and prophetic fulfillment.

There is also scientific reality in the Passover. Blood from an "unblemished" male lamb was necessary, symbolic of the Lamb of God who was without sin (unblemished), unlike any other human who ever lived. The blood had to be perfect. Normal human blood can be quite imperfect and can carry impurities, even death-causing viruses so prevalent in the world today. Only the Lamb's blood was pure, perfect, and undefiled. *Only perfect blood can perfectly cleanse.*

During this Passover meal before His death, Jesus took some bread, blessed and broke it, then gave it to His friends, saying:

"Take, eat; this is my body."[11]

Jesus' words and actions here shocked the disciples, according to Jewish authors Ceil and Moishe Rosen, because the meal, including the lamb, had already been consumed.[12] According to tradition, nothing else was to be eaten. Jesus instituted a new memorial, an after dish, later called "aphikomen." He demonstrated that the Paschal (Passover) lamb no longer had significance because the true Lamb had come. Also, Jesus apparently saw into the future when there would be no more altar (destroyed shortly thereafter by the Romans in A. D. 70) or sacrifice. He used the aphikomen for the first time to represent the Paschal lamb and *His own body*, formerly represented by the body of the animal.

The Jews have always used *unleavened* (matzo) bread for the Passover ceremony. Leaven is symbolic of sin. They use *three* matzo wafers. The *middle* one, the "aphikomen," is *broken* during the meal, *hidden*, and *later returned*. This is an early but mysterious tradition. No one really knows its meaning. The three wafers represent *unity*, but Jewish scholars do not agree on what the unity represents. Some Jews believe the three wafers represent Abraham, Isaac, and Jacob, but Isaac's body (the *middle* wafer) was never actually broken! Could it be that the unity of the three wafers represents the unity of the one but triune God (Father, *Son*, and Holy Spirit), and the *unleavened*, of course, His purity? Is the middle wafer the Son (aphikomen) whose body was indeed *broken*, who is mysteriously *hidden* from the Jewish people, and who will *return* as their Messiah as He promised? I believe it is. Such an interpretation clearly makes sense, especially in view of Jesus' own introduction of the after dish to represent His own body, plus all other Passover symbolism. Interestingly, aphikomen comes from a Greek word that is translated "the coming one," or "that which comes last."

In every Passover meal, then, the Jews albeit unknowingly celebrate the sinless Messiah whose body was broken, who temporarily is hidden, and who will return. They finish eating the broken aphikomen in the Sephardic or Eastern tradition with the words, "In memory of the Passover sacrifice." This has to be one of the most profound ceremonies in human history where, ironically, the participants do not understand the full meaning of their actions!

After Jesus broke the bread and told them to eat it, He then took a cup of wine (fruit of the vine), gave thanks, and passed it to his friends, saying:

> *"Drink of it, all of you; for this is <u>my blood of the new covenant</u>, which is poured out for many for the forgiveness of sins."*[13]
>
> *"Do this, as often as you drink it, in remembrance of me."*[14]

They were actually invited to "consume" Jesus' body and blood. This is not surprising, for as we pointed out above, the Passover lamb had been "eaten" from the beginning (later, with no lamb, the *aphikomen* was eaten instead). Previously Jesus said something puzzling to the people:

Chapter 4: The World's Greatest Substance

"Truly, truly, I say to you, unless you eat the flesh of the Son of man and drink his blood, you have no life in you; he who eats my flesh and drinks my blood has eternal life and I will raise him up at the last day."[15]

He was obviously not talking about cannibalism, but about a spiritual phenomenon. But what does it mean, and how does it work? Well, the early church replaced the prophetic Passover meal of Judaism, which was fulfilled in the Messiah, with a sacrament called "Communion," or "the Lord's Supper." Believers gathered and partook of bread (His body) and wine or grape juice (His blood) "in remembrance" of Him. The church continues that tradition today. Beliefs vary on the extent of symbolism involved in this sacrament. However one believes, it is important to participate and to remember the *cleansing and life-giving effects of the Lamb's body and blood.*

The reality of the new covenant, the eternal blood covenant, is that in the Messiah God chose to inhabit a human body, and let that body become as a sacrificial lamb, taking upon Himself the sins of the entire human population of the planet from the beginning to the end of human history. All of history and every human who ever lived or ever will live was represented on the cross with Jesus. The most profound event—ever.

Dr. Roy Blizzard, a recognized American expert in Hebrew studies and archaeology, once voiced a simple summary of this historical event for which no adjectives are adequate to describe: "In the veins of Jesus flowed God's own blood." It is a mind-boggling thought that the Creator God would choose to experience this human condition. But He purposed to do so as an *ultimate act of love.* (Note: the divine blood in Jesus' body was a result of the virgin birth, essential for the fertilized egg and resulting chromosone/gene combinations to have a divine component. Rather than myth, the virgin birth was biologically mandatory for the entire purpose of the incarnation and later crucifixion. It was a product of God's wisdom and power, and an integral and indispensable part of His plan.)

Chapter 4: The World's Greatest Substance

The Amazing "Blood-covering"

All of previous Hebrew history was but a preparation and a portrait of this divine love-plan. It didn't just start with Abraham, but can be traced all the way to the garden of Eden. When Adam and Eve disobeyed God and sinned, they used fig leaves to "cover" themselves. But God determined the mere vegetable product to be unsuitable and replaced the leaves with the skin of an animal, the first symbolic act of "blood-covering."

In this initial instance of sin, blood had to be shed to "cover" it. Surely God loved the little animal and was saddened to see its death. But He chose flesh as an atonement to demonstrate the seriousness of human sin. Sin brings human death (physical) and spiritual death (separation from God). Bloodshed typifies the seriousness of sin, because a loss of life is necessary.

But on the positive side, there is a more important reason for the blood covering. It is a medical fact that blood's most important function is to bring *life*. It is a life-giving substance rather than a symbol of death. Therefore, in addition to demonstrating the seriousness of sin, a blood sacrifice restores life to the guilty one. It covers us. It clothes us. The Bible says:

> *"And the LORD God made for Adam and his wife garments of skins, and clothed them."*[16]

An often overlooked truth in man's fall is that Adam and Eve by their own efforts had attempted to "cover" (or justify) themselves by using fig leaves. This was human reasoning causing human effort to cover human failings, a condition so prevalent in the world ever since, and especially today. But it is not God's way.

In a message also applicable to us, God said to Adam and Eve, in effect, "Your failings may be overlooked, but only *My way*. None of your self-effort can accomplish anything. You can't do anything, but I can. I will cover your sins Myself, and with blood. It is something I will do Myself. In fact, I will ultimately shed My own

Chapter 4: The World's Greatest Substance

blood for your covering. I will do that for you, because I love you." He did. That is *the blood of the eternal covenant.*[17]

The "Lost" Ark of the Covenant

The subject of the popular movie, "Raiders of the Lost Ark," was the famous ark of the covenant that the Israelites used according to God's instructions. The ark provided further prophetic symbolism of the eternal blood covenant to come. It was a box that contained the original tablets of the Ten Commandments. It was kept in the Holy of Holies behind a curtain in the Holy Place both of the tabernacle and the later temple. This is the place where God manifested a special presence—the most holy of places, ever (until God later chose a different type of temple in which to reveal Himself as described in Chapter 8).

The top of the box was called the Mercy Seat (Hebrew word for "cover"). The sins of the people were covered, or forgiven, once a year when the high priest would sprinkle the blood of sacrificed animals on the Mercy Seat.[18] In effect, the Commandments within the ark were declaring the guilt of the people before the presence of God. But the blood on the Mercy Seat "covered" the accusations before they could even reach God!

The New Testament fulfillment of this symbolism was the Messiah, called the great high priest, whose own sacrifice is the "covering" for sins. The Commandments still declare our guilt, as no one can keep them perfectly by letter or spirit. But the blood of the eternal covenant "covers" the accusations. Such covering renders a "not guilty" verdict before God for those who have entered into the covenant, just like in the Old Testament practice.

(What really happened to the "lost" ark, the subject of the aforementioned movie? It actually disappeared in history and hasn't been seen since. I believe I have discovered the ark's location and why it hasn't been found! See Appendix II for this fascinating information).

Chapter 4: The World's Greatest Substance

How to Enter into the Covenant

How does one enter into the covenant? By *faith*—"consuming" this truth within ourselves. As we do so, we "eat" His flesh and "drink" His blood, consuming the Passover Lamb, just like the early Israelites consumed the slain lamb. The Lamb and His blood give us life and cleanse us from all of sin's impurities. We enter into an irrevocable covenant with God Almighty who has promised eternal life: "I will raise him up at the last day."

> *"For God so loved the world that he gave his only Son, that whoever believes in him should not perish but have eternal life."*[19]

God demonstrated this love by shedding His own blood, through which He made a covenant. We enter into this covenant by "believing" in Him and what He did. The words *faith* and *believing* mean more than just intellectual agreement; rather they carry the idea of "relying on," and "trusting in." Basically, it means to entrust ourselves to God, an act of commitment. We "covenant" with Him. He gave His life to us; we give our life to Him. And in a mystery to be discussed in Chapter 8, the blood covenant brings an inter-union of the two covenant makers.

It took God centuries of human history to orchestrate the events leading to the enactment of the blood covenant. But a person can enter into it in a moment, whether 10 years old or 110. In only One Minute or less. Sudden insight into Truth—a spark of faith—an inner acceptance and commitment. Shazam! That's just the way it works. (Follow-through? See Chapters 8-12.) When we do, we are no longer captive to an existence constantly stalked by death. Everything in this world dies. All flesh decomposes, as does all vegetation. Even the sun has a limited life and is gradually dying. But we have found real and permanent life through that life-giving substance, blood—a special and very unusual blood:

> *"You were ransomed* (Webster: freed from captivity or punishment by paying a price)....*with the precious blood*

Chapter 4: The World's Greatest Substance

of Christ (Messiah), like that of a lamb without blemish or spot."[20]

Interestingly, it was through Judaism and the Old Covenant that God instituted blood sacrifice as a means of removing sin and guilt. But when Messiah, the Lamb of God, finally came, He became a final and lasting sacrifice for all time. Coincidentally, in the first century, animal sacrifice ceased in Judaism. Although ostensibly for naturally explainable reasons, God obviously had a profound spiritual reason—its prophetic purpose had been fulfilled.

This leaves a troubling problem for those who would reject Yeshua (Jesus) as the sacrificial Lamb. The first-century writer of the Letter to the Hebrews reminded them that:

"without the shedding of blood there is no forgiveness of sins."[21]

Nowhere in the Jewish Scriptures did God change His mind and decide that blood was no longer required as a sin sacrifice. It always was, and still is, required. But the old symbolic way ceased. Now, for Jews and Gentiles, there is still a blood covering through the "blood of the new covenant." God appeared in human form to sacrifice His own flesh one time, only one time, and for all time. He did it not just for the Jews who were the "chosen people" to communicate and implement His plan, but for all people, Jews and Gentiles of every nation, everywhere.

Even God's real name describes this incredible love-mission. It is really "the world's greatest name." This fascinating and mysterious subject is discussed in the next chapter.

`00:01:00`

ONE MINUTE SUMMARY
The World's Greatest Substance

Blood is a miraculous and life-giving substance. In an incredibly complex 60,000 mile network of vessels, blood delivers food to every one of our one hundred trillion cells. Then, on the return trip it picks up waste for disposal, literally "washing" each cell. Without this constant food supply, we could not live. Without this constant removal of waste, we would die from poisoning. Amazingly, thousands of years ago, before any scientific knowledge of the body existed, the Bible writers said that "the life of the flesh is in the blood," and that the blood of Messiah *washes* and *cleanses* us. The latter statement was made at a time when blood was thought of as something that only soiled or stained. God apparently chose blood to represent *life* and also to demonstrate death, the consequence of sin, unless "washed" away or "cleansed" by the blood of his Son.

From the Garden of Eden throughout the Old Testament (Covenant), blood sacrifice represented a covering or cleansing for human sin. It prophetically and symbolically pointed toward the coming Messiah, the Lamb of God, who would be sacrificed as a substitutional punishment for all humans who ever lived. At the last meal before His execution, the Passover meal, Jesus said that His blood was the "blood of the new covenant." He also said that consuming this blood, or truth, (by faith) into our spirits gives us eternal *life*. Like human blood does physically—giving life and washing away poisons, Jesus' blood does spiritually—giving spiritual life and washing away spiritual poisons.

CHAPTER FIVE

The World's Greatest Name

Chapter 5: The World's Greatest Name

There is only one name in all of history so revered and so feared that millions of people would not even utter it, and still don't. Because of that, it has been called "the Incommunicable Name" and "the Great and Terrible Name."

This "unutterable word," as it is also called, is the Creator's actual name as He revealed it to Moses some 1,500 years before Christ. No wonder it has been feared—the warning against profaning it occupies a full ten percent of the Decalogue, or Ten Commandments:

> *"You shall not take the name of _____ your God in vain; for _____ will not hold him guiltless who takes his name in vain."*[1]

That stern command and the consequence of disobedience is enough to make any rational person nervous!

What awesome name goes into the above blank spaces? Strangely, most Christians today do not know what it is, and Jews generally still will not pronounce it, instead substituting another word. It is undoubtedly the greatest mystery of name and word usage in history.

The Creator's name is not "God" (from the Hebrew "El" or "Elohim"). God is really a generic word used also in the Bible for pagan deities. His name is not "Lord." This is also a generic word meaning "master," the same word that is also used to refer to human masters. In both cases, distinction is attempted by capitalization. But the Creator did not give Himself a name to be shared with pagan deities or humans, even with capitalization. Actually, God and Lord are more titles and not names. Neither is His name "Jehovah," a word invention of late medieval origin. Strangely, Jehovah is still popularly but mistakenly used as the Creator's name even though scholars and seminary graduates have known for years that it is incorrect.

Chapter 5: The World's Greatest Name

The Creator's actual name is unique and exclusive, not shared with any other being. Its origin is from the beginning of time, and its meaning, as we shall see, is descriptive of the nature of its owner. And it is a fascinating fact that the mystery surrounding the name was apparently anticipated by early Hebrew Scripture itself. Hundreds of years before Christ, the mystery of the name was referred to in the Proverbs. After describing the Creator's mighty power, it teasingly asks:

> "What is his name, and what is his son's name, if thou canst tell?"[2]

Other translations say, "Tell me if you know!" or "Surely you know!" This amazing verse not only infers a riddle associated with the Creator's name but prophetically refers to the name of the Son who was not even born yet! And the Son's name, too, is somewhat of a mystery.

What Is His Name?

Well, what is it? What is the name that has struck fear in the hearts of millions of people for thousands of years, and still does?

The Creator revealed His name in the Hebrew language; it appears more than 6,000 times in the Old Testament. Here it is:

יהוה

Reading from right to left, as is done in Hebrew, it contains the four consonants, Y H W H. Scholars call these famous four letters the "Tetragrammaton" (*tetra* for *four*). Though its pronunciation was long obscure, there is now almost general agreement among scholars that the correct vowel insertions should be Y*a*HW*e*H, making the actual and original name *Yahweh*. The short form, *Yah*, appears in "Hallelujah" (meaning "praise you, Yah"—the j strangely inserted about three centuries ago), a universal praise word spoken by people of many languages all over the world.

Chapter 5: The World's Greatest Name

Sometimes people use Hallelujah carelessly and without knowledge of its meaning or profound implications. I once heard it in a TV soft drink commercial. Humanity's ignorance and disregard of sacred truth is sad and frightening.

On one occasion God spoke through the prophet, Isaiah, and said very pointedly:

"I am 'Yahweh,' that is my name!"[3]

And after He had revealed His name to Moses, God said:

"This is my name forever, the name by which I am to be remembered from generation to generation."[4]

Has humanity complied with that command to remember? Apparently not. That's the purpose of this chapter. After you read it you will know something of great spiritual and historical significance, and hopefully of great personal value and blessing.

Why the Greatest Name Was Almost Lost

The problem started in Old Testament times when the Rabbis, fearful of violating the commandment and even inadvertently profaning the sacred name, overreacted and eliminated its use altogether in temple worship by substituting another word. Even today, thousands of years later, when Jews see the Hebrew word, YHWH, they automatically pronounce it "Adonai," the word for "Lord." Curious about the practice, I have asked Jewish acquaintances why they still do this. One admitted that he was superstitious. Another replied, "We are not 100% sure that 'Yahweh' is the correct pronunciation of YHWH." He preferred a word we know as 100% wrong to one we know is probably 99% right!

I include this to demonstrate the deep roots of tradition and superstition, but not to be critical. Their reverence is admirable, certainly more so than the flippant attitude often given to matters of deity by many Gentiles.

Chapter 5: The World's Greatest Name

This practice of substitution continued when the Hebrew Scriptures were translated into Greek, and centuries later into English. Most modern Bibles today follow this practice and substitute "the LORD" (all caps) for the Creator's name, even while admitting it is wrong. For example, the introduction to the *New English Bible* (Oxford University Press) says:

> *"In course of time, the true pronunciation of the divine name, probably 'Yahweh,' passed into oblivion and YHWH was read with the intruded vowels, the vowels of an entirely different word, namely 'my Lord' or 'God'...the present translators have retained this <u>incorrect</u> but customary form."*

In some Bibles, the mighty name is mentioned as a footnote, such as *The Living Bible* (Tyndale House Publishers). It comments on its use of "Jehovah" in Exodus 3:14 by adding in small print, "Properly the name should be pronounced 'Yahweh.'"

The *Criswell Study Bible* (Thomas Nelson Publishers) footnote on the same verse says, "YAHWEH....(is) the personal name of God."

First Century Status of the Name

What was the status of the sacred name during the time of Christ? The Jewish Encyclopedia quotes the first-century philosopher, Philo:

> *"The four letters may be mentioned or heard only by holy men whose ears and tongues are purified by wisdom, and by no others in any place whatsoever."*

First-century Jewish and Roman historian Josephus wrote:

> *"Moses besought God to impart to him the knowledge of His name and its pronunciation so that he might be able to invoke Him by name at the sacred acts, whereupon God communicated His name, hitherto unknown to any man; and it would be a sin for me to mention it."*

Apparently, by the time of Christ the name had virtually been removed from use in Judaism. This may help explain what Jesus meant when He prayed:

> "I have manifested thy name to the men whom thou gavest me....I made known to them thy name."[5]

Actually, an early messianic prophecy fulfilled by Jesus said:

> "I will declare thy name unto my brethren."[6]

Of course, these statements may have a broader meaning than just that of declaring the sacred name, Yahweh. They also probably mean the declaration of God's total Person to the world.

And What Is His Son's Name?

This is the other question asked by the writer of Proverbs hundreds of years before Christ came. While we are almost certain of the name "Yahweh," the name of the Son is less certain, although we have some good clues.

The problem is that we know it was a Hebrew name, but the New Testament records are in Greek. These not only followed tradition and changed YHWH to the word for "Lord," but also changed the Son's name to a Greek word, Iesous (pronounced ee-ay-sooce). In English it later became "Jesus," an Anglicized rendering of the Greek. Jesus is a beautiful name to which most people are accustomed, but it is a relatively recent derivation. It did not even appear in the original King James Version of the Bible in 1611 which contained no "J," a recent letter of the alphabet, all of which may surprise many.

So, His real name was not Jesus, nor was His last name Christ. Actually, Christ is from the Greek word for the Hebrew "Messiah," a title which confirms His deity, but not a name. Christ and Messiah mean the same.

Chapter 5: The World's Greatest Name

But what did his mother Mary call him, and his friends? Well, we know from Matthew 1:21 that the angel's announcement conveyed the meaning of "salvation." There is general agreement, therefore, that the last part of his name is "shua" from the Hebrew word for salvation. His actual name is normally rendered as "Yeshua," or simply "Y'shua." Scholarly references usually include an expanded form, "Yehoshua," which is also the name given to Joshua (Numbers 13:16). Strangely, Jesus and Joshua have the same Hebrew name, transliterated the same in the Greek, sometimes even used interchangeably, but they are rendered differently in English. Many scholars believe that Joshua was an Old Testament symbol, or forerunner, of Jesus; he led his people to the promised land, or place of blessing.

Yehoshua is translated "Yahweh is salvation," or "Yahweh saves." It contains the first three letters, YHW, of the four-consonant divine name, the Tetragrammaton (fine points of Hebrew grammar change letter sounds in pronunciation). In the Old Testament, a suffix was frequently added to the name Yahweh to indicate His provision for humanity's needs, such as Yahweh-Shalom (Yahweh is peace). The central message of the New Testament is that Yahweh Himself appeared in the flesh for humanity's salvation. It is logical and consistent that He would carry the same name but with the added meaning of His mission and purpose—human salvation.

The connection between the Old Testament Yahweh and the New Testament Jesus (Yehoshua) is often missed even by otherwise informed students. For example, the real meaning of the popular verses Romans 10:9 and I Corinthians 12:3, where both use the same expression, "Jesus is LORD," is not always understood properly. The expression is often thought of as meaning confessing Jesus as "Master" of one's life. But in possibly the most profound footnote ever written in any book, the *New International Version Study Bible* (Zondervan Bible Publishers) points out:

> *"The Greek word for "LORD" here is used in the Greek translation of the Old Testament (the Septuagint) to translate the Hebrew name Yahweh."*

The popular confession of "Jesus is LORD" really means, but was lost in translations, *"Jesus is Yahweh"*—that He was the God of the Old Testament in human form! An incredibly profound truth (and according to I Corinthians 12:3 such insight can only come from a revelation by the Holy Spirit). These passages become compatible with other Bible principles that stress *grace* and *faith* as triggering salvation instead of human works. The "LORD" or "Master" meaning implies that salvation is dependent upon human works—"allowing" Jesus to be the absolute Master of one's life. This is an ideal we should all strive for, but, realistically, no one achieves it absolutely. If a criterion for salvation, no one would qualify because without grace, God's requirement for performance is absolute, not partial.

Can you see that "Jesus—or Yehoshua (Yahweh saves)—is Yahweh?" If so, that is evidence that you have personally received divine revelation.

Is God's Name Important?

Many sincere scholars believe that it is not important to know and use the Creator's actual name, Yahweh. For example, the Editorial Board of the *New American Standard Bible* (The Lockman Foundation) explains why they omitted it:

> *"This name conveys no religious or spiritual overtones. It is strange, uncommon, and without sufficient religious and devotional background."*

But this view is not unanimous. The popular and respected *Smith's Bible Dictionary* (Fleming H. Revell Company) says:

> *"The substitution of the word LORD is most unhappy; for, while it in no way represents the meaning of the sacred name, the mind has constantly to guard against its lower uses, and above all, the direct personal bearing of the name on the revelation of God through the whole course of Jewish history is kept injuriously out of sight."*

Chapter 5: The World's Greatest Name

It should be mentioned that "Yahweh" is used instead of "the LORD" in the popular Catholic *Jerusalem Bible*, (Doubleday and Company).

Is God's name really important? You must decide in view of the Scriptures and the many human opinions, including mine. Here are some more thoughts.

Is your name important? A name identifies its owner. It's a personal thing. And a relationship is difficult without the use of personal names. How would you like it for those you love the most to never call you by your name, or not even know it, calling you something else? You would still love them but the relationship would lack a degree of intimacy.

The name Yahweh actually contains the nature of God: its root meaning in Hebrew is that of self-derived eternal existence as well as, according to some linguists, causation, changelessness, and eternal presence. Thus, the name is holy. In what we call "the Lord's Prayer," Jesus taught us to pray, "Hallowed be thy name" (the very *first* and thereby perhaps highest priority phrase of the prayer). Many of us have done this thousands of times without even knowing what the name is!

There are scores of references to the sacred name in the Bible with exhortations to bless it, praise it, exalt it, and use it. Here are a few:

"Bless Yahweh....bless his holy name!"[7]

"O Yahweh....how majestic is thy name in all the earth!"[8]

"Let us exalt his name together!"[9]

"Sing praises to his name....his name is Yah."[10]

"Thy name is as ointment poured forth."[11]

"Let them also that love thy name be joyful in thee."[12]

Here is a blessing that many have discovered, a way to increase the intimacy of your relationship with your Creator. When you talk

Chapter 5: The World's Greatest Name

to Him in prayer, call Him by His personal name. Some people report a reality never before experienced. And here's a wonderful and scriptural exercise for you. In Hebrew the word "bless" (barak) literally means "to adore on bended knee." Implement that first verse above ("Bless Yahweh....bless his holy name") by bending your knees and saying to your Creator, "I adore you, Yahweh....I adore your holy name."

There are some cultic groups that use the name of Yahweh but deny much of the Bible's teachings. But cults also use the terms "Jehovah," "Lord," and "Jesus," so don't let that discourage you from knowing and using your Creator's name. See Chapter 11 on how to recognize a false cult.

In conclusion, I hope this message duplicates for you the effects of Moses' own declaration of the "Great and Terrible Name," as he described it:

"My teaching shall drop as the rain, my speech shall distil as the dew....because I will publish the name of Yahweh."[13]

00:01:00

ONE MINUTE SUMMARY
The World's Greatest Name

It is the most revered, most feared, and most mysterious name in the history of the world and is referred to as the "Incommunicable Name." It is so revered and feared that millions of people have refused to even pronounce it. Because of disuse, the mysterious name was almost lost in antiquity. Other words have been substituted for it in both ancient and modern documents. Most Bibles still avoid its use. A warning against its misuse occupies a full ten percent of the Ten Commandments. It is the name of the Creator of the universe, revealed to Moses some 3,500 years ago.

The holy name is: YHWH. For centuries the correct pronunciation has been obscure, but scholars are now almost certain that the proper vowel insertions render the name as "Yahweh." Due to overreaction to the stern wording of the commandment and fear of inadvertently profaning the sacred name, ancient rabbis eliminated its use altogether in temple worship. This began a tradition of word substitution for the Creator's name which continues today. When Jews see YHWH in Hebrew, they pronounce it "Adonai," the word for "Lord." Most English Bibles follow this tradition and translate YHWH as "the LORD." Jesus' real name is "Yeshua," or the expanded "Yehoshua," meaning "Yahweh is salvation." "Christ" is not his last name, but is from the Greek word for the Hebrew "Messiah," his title. The New Testament reveals that "Jesus is LORD." Technically, however, the word "LORD" should be rendered "Yahweh," making the profound statement that *Jesus was the God of the Old Testament in human form,* the most astounding fact in human history. The sacred name itself is an additional portrait of the incredible incarnation.

Chapter 5: The World's Greatest Name

"I will make thy name to be remembered."
Psalm 45:17

CHAPTER SIX

The World's Greatest Message

Chapter 6: The World's Greatest Message

It's called the *"message* of reconciliation." This is really one of those "bad news - good news" situations. Here is what it is all about.

You are a created being and obviously physical in nature. But you are keenly aware that there is something more than that—you know there is also a nonmaterial or "spirit" nature. You really don't know where you came from, except from the inside of your mother. But that doesn't really answer the question: "What's this crazy life all about?" You know that there is a God, but He is distant and unfamiliar. You sense a separation between God and yourself. There is, indeed, a separation, evidenced by the fact that you have to ask these questions. That's the "bad news."

You wonder:

What is God like?
What does He think about me?
Can I know Him?
Will I ever see Him?
What happens to the real me after my body dies, which it someday will?

Well, there is one place in the whole world, and only one place, where there is an answer to these seemingly impossible questions—the Bible. And the answer is the "good news." That's actually the definition of the familiar word, *gospel*: a "good message" or "good news." While this good news had been a secret for long ages (see Chapter 3), Jesus' main instructions to His disciples before He ascended into heaven was for His followers to "go into all the world and tell this good news." That's why people who have heard it want to tell others about it.

It's like finding a cure for cancer and being unable to keep it to yourself! It's not proselyting in the sense of recruiting members (although some may be guilty of that); instead it's like shouting the news of rescue to fellow inhabitants on a lost space ship. And aren't we?

Yes, there is a separation (the bad news), but there is also reconciliation (the good news). In fact, the apostle Paul says in the Bible:

Chapter 6: The World's Greatest Message

> *"God was in Christ reconciling the world to himself... and entrusting to us the <u>message of reconciliation</u>. So we are ambassadors for Christ, God making his appeal through us."*[1]

This *good news* message of reconciliation is "the world's greatest message."

The Reason For Separation

Why is there separation in the first place? And why is reconciliation necessary? Well, it's really simple when you stop to think about it. It's totally logical. The Bible reveals God as pure and holy—absolute perfection without even a single trace of any vice—a perfect Being. Like the famous old hymn says:

> *"Holy, Holy, Holy! Though the darkness hide Thee,*
> *Though the eye of sinful man Thy glory may not see.*
> *Only Thou art holy, there is none beside Thee,*
> *Perfect in power, in love, and purity.*[2]

Humanity, on the other hand, is imperfect. All of us fall short of perfect love, and purity of intent and actions. While few of us may be murderers, rapists, or thieves (at least of big things), nevertheless any rational person will admit that he or she is not perfect. Even the most saintly human knows his "bad side." We all have it. Come on. Admit it. Some people, of course, choose a consistent and blatantly immoral "lifestyle" (a word currently popular so the behavior won't sound so bad; rarely used to mean a moral life). Consequently, if God's perfection represents 100% on the scale, all of us fall somewhere between 0 and 99 (technically, according to the Bible, we all score a big "zip," zero, as they say in sports—our own purity in comparison with God's). *The problem*: In God's eyes, only 100% is passing! God's perfect nature demands no less than an absolute standard. Unfortunately, according to His standard of perfection, we all flunk. That's the bad news.

Chapter 6: The World's Greatest Message

The Unbridgeable Chasm

There is a great chasm separating God and humanity. Nothing man can do can bridge that chasm. However, in man's pride and ignorance he thinks he can cross the chasm separating himself from God. Many try good deeds, community service, philanthropy, even religion, trying to "justify" themselves before God and make Him their debtor. Some even attend or "join" churches or synagogues without an understanding of what it is all about. Ask many Christians and Jews what they believe and why they believe it and they are not at all sure. These activities are not evil in themselves unless they are viewed as self-righteous efforts to "earn" God's favor. But "activities" or "joining" anything does not ameliorate the root problem, nor do they bridge the unbridgeable chasm to God's holiness.

Only the Bible explains humanity's propensity for evil, tracing this tendency all the way back to the very first humans. It has to do with the free exercise of our wills. Sometimes, even though we know better, we "will" to do wrong, to say or do something that may not honor God or may hurt someone else, violating God's principle attribute and the basic law of the universe—love. We just do it, like an incorrigible kid. Any such behavior is called "sin."

What person would deny that there is evil in the world? Who can look at history and witness man's inhumanity to man, and not admit the reality of evil. The problem is not just among nations, but within cities; even between neighbors, and within families. A person, who with philosophic ease might deny the reality of evil, would rapidly change his mind if a loved one was raped or killed, or if he had to experience Hitler's death camps. Some who reject God's truths say that education is the answer to all this, a panacea brought about, of course, by more government spending. Secular mentality often views government as god, a modern form of idolatry. However, some of the most evil deeds are done by some of the most educated people. And Hitler's Germany was one of the most "civilized" and educated nations in the history of the world.

On a smaller scale, what about a harsh word to someone which causes hurt and maybe a permanent scar? What honest person would deny that there is occasionally evil in all of us, ranging from mildly

Chapter 6: The World's Greatest Message

selfish thoughts and deeds to deeds that can severely hurt others. There is some evil in every person. Actually, the totality of the evil of the self-centeredness of the average, apparently well-meaning person, any of us, would probably be shocking if we could see it with God's eyes. Admit it or not, we are all morally flawed—imperfect. Like oil and water, perfection and imperfection cannot mix. The two are distinct and separated.

Yet fellowship and reconciliation are God's heart desires. He originally created humans for the purpose of a mutual love relationship, and that is His ideal plan for eternity. You might say that His attribute of love actually caused the creation of humans. Why? Because love is not just a mushy feeling. *Love demands an object*; it is an active, not a passive concept. God's creation is the object of His love and a way in which He can express His love, putting it into action.

"Then why doesn't He just look over my imperfections and accept me the way I am?" Well, in a sense that's exactly what He does. That's the good news! There's only one requirement. God cannot deny His own nature, and the universe must work on consistent principles. An important part of God's nature is *justice*. Justice must always be served. This is an eternal and spiritual principle. There is *always* judgment, without exception. Nothing escapes God's awareness and justice. This means our wrongdoing, no matter the degree, small or large, must be dealt with. It must receive recompense. The recompense, or reward, of wrongdoing is separation from God, the only source of good, joy, and true happiness in the universe. To be "cutoff" from God is an unimaginable horror.

The scheme of eternity would be out of whack and unfair if evil was just ignored and not recompensed. Like the law of physics, an action requires a reaction. The action of man's self-centeredness and propensity for evil has already, in fact, produced the reaction—*there already is separation*, and without a solution it will remain that way forever. Humanity in general is already "cutoff" from God. For proof, check your local newspaper, a daily documentation of a lost species.

Chapter 6: The World's Greatest Message

God's Dilemma?

"But how terrible," you may say. "I don't want to be punished for any wrong I have done. I don't want to be 'cutoff' from God. Where is His mercy?" Is there a conflict between God's attributes of love and mercy and His attribute of justice? This may seem true in our human way of thinking, but the seeming conflict in attributes is actually what produced the answer—His attributes of perfect *justice* and *wisdom*, combined with His attribute of perfect *love*.

In effect, God said, "There is only one way where both love and justice can be served, where My actions will be consistent and true as they must be. I will take their punishment on Myself. Yes, that's it! I will take on human form and suffer for them. I will come as a Son and be their substitute. All they will have to do is to acknowledge what I have done for them. Then justice will be served. If they will just believe Me and accept what I will do for them, then I will declare them as righteous in My eyes, just as though they are perfect as I am. That is My covenant with them, and I will seal this covenant in My own blood."

God then revealed this plan through His Hebrew prophets. For example, Isaiah wrote about the perfect One to come in the future:

> "*He was wounded for our transgressions, he was bruised for our iniquities...like a lamb that is led to the slaughter...by his knowledge shall...(he) make many to be accounted righteous.*"[3]

The Chasm Is Bridged

This prophecy was fulfilled about 700 years later. Yeshua (Jesus) came and revealed that He was the fulfillment of the writings of Isaiah and all the other prophets. He summarized His mission when He said:

> "*For God so loved the world that he gave his only Son, that whoever believes in him should not perish but have eternal life.*"[4]

Chapter 6: The World's Greatest Message

Out of love, God Himself bridged the chasm that man could not bridge. Religion is sometimes defined as man trying to reach to God, trying to cross the impossible chasm. But in Christ, God reached down to man, doing for man what he could not do for himself. Fellowship with God requires "righteousness," or purity, on our part; but even after commitment to Christ our own good works and deeds are insufficient. The only righteousness God sees as pure and acceptable is that of His Son. Nothing else will work. God "imputes" or gives His Son's righteousness to those who place their faith in Him. Though undeserved, He "credits" us with His Son's righteousness.

Essentially, that is the gospel, the good news—the greatest message and the greatest love story the world has ever heard. It is also "the world's greatest secret" previously described in Chapter 3. This is the message of reconciliation, the message of *grace*, maybe the most wonderful word in the entire Bible. Remember that word, *grace*. Meditate on it. Savor it. It means "unmerited favor," or receiving something good that you do not deserve. It is the subject of one of the greatest hymns ever written. Believers for over 200 years have been singing:

> *Amazing grace, how sweet the sound,*
> *That saved a wretch like me.*
> *I once was lost, but now am found —*
> *was blind but now I see.*
> *'Twas grace that taught my heart to fear*
> *And grace my fears relieved.*
> *How precious did that grace appear*
> *The* <u>*hour*</u> *I first believed.*[5]

In case you have never done so, this can be your *hour*. You can receive that same grace, right now—actually in just One Minute—if you believe, just like the song says.

For thousands of years this message, when heard, has resulted in "the world's greatest experience," the subject of the next chapter.

00:01:00

ONE MINUTE SUMMARY
The World's Greatest Message

Many people wonder about God. Where is He? Some are so oblivious to His existence that they have declared Him "dead." This speaks of their own condition more than God's. Most people know and admit that He exists but sense a separation from Him. That is a valid feeling, because the Bible declares that there is, indeed, a separation between God and humanity. Actually, a chasm exists that man cannot bridge. It is because of God's purity and holiness and man's impure and imperfect nature. Like oil and water, the two natures cannot mix. Nothing man can do, such as good works and good intentions, will enable him to bridge the chasm. Only God can bridge it. And He did it through his Son. "Religion," generally, is man trying to reach up to God. But in Christ, God reached down to man.

God is just. Sin must always be recompensed. But God is also love. To be consistent with His own attributes, God wisely chose a method to "reconcile" humanity to Himself that would not contradict His nature. He would become our substitute and take our punishment Himself, thus bridging the chasm for those who would accept His sacrifice and act of substitution. He would become a Son and suffer death for every human. This amazing plan was foretold through the Hebrew prophets. All the prophecies were fulfilled in Yeshua (Jesus), who summarized this *message* of reconciliation when He said:

> "For God so loved the world that he gave his only Son, that whoever believes in him should not perish but have eternal life."

CHAPTER SEVEN

The World's Greatest Experience

Chapter 7: The World's Greatest Experience

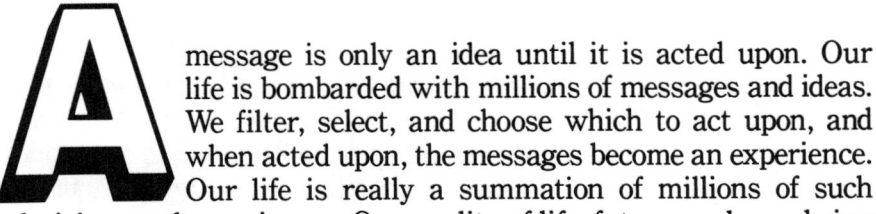

A message is only an idea until it is acted upon. Our life is bombarded with millions of messages and ideas. We filter, select, and choose which to act upon, and when acted upon, the messages become an experience. Our life is really a summation of millions of such decisions and experiences. Our quality of life, future, and very being are determined by the messages we choose to act upon. There is one experience, however, that exceeds and transcends them all. Nothing can compare with it. It is really "the world's greatest experience."

This chapter will give you real-life examples of this experience. Actually, these are even "the world's greatest examples," classic examples taken from the pages of the Bible. One absolutely amazing common trait is that *they all took about one minute or less*! I was shocked when I discovered this incredible fact. I even confirmed it with my stopwatch. It's true. And it's more good news for you—you can have the same experience in *one minute* or less!

The first two examples are found in the Old Testament and occurred before Christ came. They represent types, or prophetic symbols, of the "good news" that was to come through the Messiah. The others are recorded in the New Testament. In all these cases, people heard a "message," responded to it, and in about one minute or less became recipients of God's *grace*, or "unmerited favor."

Old Testament Examples

CASE 1

Four thousand years ago lived the first Hebrew. He was the father of the Hebrew people, named Abram, later called Abraham. God chose Abram for a great purpose. God spoke to Abram in a vision and revealed His plans with him.[1]

The vision and their conversation, as described, took less than one minute. Within the same one minute, Abram did something that instantly gave him *grace*. It is written:

Chapter 7: The World's Greatest Experience

> *"He (Abram) believed the Lord; and he reckoned it to him as righteousness."*[2]

This is one of the most profound statements in the Bible, and one of the first of many examples of what theologians call "justification by faith." In a nutshell, it means that people can stand before the perfect and omnipotent Creator, justified (in good standing) by an act of faith, regardless of what they may have done in their life. "Justified" is actually a judicial term meaning "declared not guilty." The term, "reckoned" above, sometimes translated "credited," is actually an accounting term. "Righteousness" is placed as a free gift in the credit side of our life's ledger, with the debit side cancelled. Some people like to believe that someday God will look at the "balance" of the credit and debit sides, and we'll be okay if the former is larger than the latter. But it doesn't work that way. The ledger will either be all credit (put there by God) or all debit (our own efforts).

This grace comes by faith, and nothing else can do it—not by membership in any organization or church, not by a lifetime of good works no matter how sincere or zealous or sacrificial, not by being a good mother or father, not by being active in the community, and certainly not by one's position in society or net worth.

Justification and grace *by faith*. This is an Old Covenant example of a New Covenant reality. In the New Testament Paul refers to what happened to Abraham and explains how the same principle is also applicable to us today:

> *"But the words, 'It was reckoned to him,' were not written for his sake alone, but for ours also...who believe in him that raised from the dead Jesus our Lord, who was put to death for our trespasses and raised for our justification."*[3]

Paul also reiterated the principle in another famous passage:

"For by grace you have been saved through faith; and this is not your own doing, it is a gift of God—not because of works, lest any man should boast."[4]

CASE 2

Over 3,000 years ago, the Israelites were captive in Egypt. Through Moses God warned them about a scourge of death to come upon the Egyptians. To protect them from this scourge, God gave them a procedure to follow that would take about one minute. God said if they would obey Him and follow the procedure He would "pass over" them, exempting them from this death.[5]

They were obedient, and God did pass over them. The Jews have celebrated this "Passover" ever since, as we discussed in an earlier chapter. This simple act of faith and One Minute Procedure were the key to the Israelites' liberation from Egyptian bondage. They could now enter the "promised land" that God had prepared for them. There is great symbolism in this event, especially the One Minute Procedure.

What was the procedure? Remember, the blood of an unblemished, or perfect, *male lamb* was to be put upon their doorposts. By doing this, God promised, the Israelites would be spared from punishment. An important point and principle is that they were spared not because of how "good" they were, or not because of their religious works, or their own righteousness. They were spared only because *they applied the blood*, regardless of their past deeds.

Remember, this was about 1,500 years before Jesus, the Messiah, came. Can you see the symbolism? Jesus, of course, was an unblemished, perfect male lamb—the Lamb of God. *When, by faith, we apply His blood to the doorposts of our hearts, God sees it and "passes over" us in dispensing eternal justice*, regardless of our past deeds.

New Testament Examples
CASE 3

There once was a man who led an evil life. He was a confirmed and self-confessed criminal. The man was being executed for his

Chapter 7: The World's Greatest Experience

crimes and had only moments to live. He probably had done few, if any, good works for the benefit of mankind. As God looked upon this criminal's ledger of life, it was undoubtedly all bad—everything on the "debit" side. The evil man was hanging by his own flesh from a bloody Roman cross. It must have been a horrible sight. Bystanders were probably saying, "He's getting what he deserves." And he was.

If there was any justice in the universe, this man did not deserve mercy from a holy God, especially the exalted privilege of eternal habitation with Him. Surely this privilege was only for the "good" people.

But a strange thing happened. Nearby Jesus was also being executed and near death on a Roman cross. The wretched man called out to Him, "Jesus, remember me when you come in your kingly power."

In that short and simple cry, the criminal may not have realized all that he actually had said. (1) He obviously acknowledged Jesus' deity, (2) he expressed faith in Jesus, and (3) he asked for mercy. His action took less than one minute—actually only about five seconds!

Divine justice for this criminal was swift. It was a different kind of justice, but the kind this book is about. Jesus replied, "Truly, I say to you, today you will be with Me in Paradise."[6]

Jesus was judge and jury. He didn't have to consult the record of legal precedent. He didn't have to take a public opinion poll. What He did do, however, was to take a guilty man and declare him not guilty, or justified. This criminal had not only broken the laws of man but also the laws of God. But in eternity, he had been declared "not guilty," because of his faith in the Son of God.

There was a second criminal in the drama who apparently did not qualify for acquittal; his guilt remained. One criminal was declared not guilty; the other remained guilty. One went to Paradise; the other didn't. A strange kind of justice? Not really. Actually, Jesus did invoke legal precedent. He implemented a divine law, or principle, that He Himself was in the process of ratifying by His own death, as we have described.

Chapter 7: The World's Greatest Experience

But where was love as far as this second criminal was concerned? At that very moment, right before the criminal's eyes, the greatest love story in the history of the world was being enacted. But he refused to see it. And today, just like then, some see, while others refuse to see, even though it is right in front of them.

CASE 4

On the day of the Pentecost observance, shortly after Jesus' death and resurrection almost 2,000 years ago, the apostle Peter began speaking to a crowd of people, mostly Jews, in Jerusalem. He explained to them what had recently happened regarding Jesus. The crowd was so moved and "cut to the heart" by his words that they cried out, "What shall we do?"

Peter responded with just a few words that took considerably less than one minute, actually more like about 15 seconds. He said:

"Repent, and be baptized every one of you in the name of Jesus Christ for the forgiveness of your sins; and you shall receive the gift of the Holy Spirit."[7]

The "gift of the Holy Spirit" is God Himself—His spirit. He literally gives us His own life when we "repent" (literally: change our mind and direction and turn to Him in faith).

The crowd's response also took less than one minute. And it is recorded that *on that very day, about 3,000 people received God's grace as a free gift!*

CASE 5

The scene was the home of an officer in the Roman army, a centurion named Cornelius. He had gathered some relatives and friends together to hear the apostle Peter tell "all that you have been commanded by the Lord."

Peter began speaking and continued for only about one minute. Then all of a sudden "while Peter was still saying this," the grace of God was given in a dramatic way to all the listeners.[8]

Chapter 7: The World's Greatest Experience

CASE 6

Paul and Silas had been thrown in jail for proclaiming this incredible message about God's grace. When an earthquake suddenly shook the prison, opened the doors and freed the prisoners, the jailer became terrified at the display of divine power surrounding Paul and Silas. He fell at their feet and cried out, "Men, what must I do to be saved."

Paul and Silas did not respond with the modern technique of nondirective counseling where you answer a question with another question saying, "Well, what do you think?" (helping the subject to hopefully stumble upon the truth). Neither did they recommend membership in any particular organization, along with accompanying rites and rituals. Nor did they pull out a big book to explain and expound on theology and metaphysics.

Instead they gave the jailer a One Minute Message—actually only 14 words, taking only about five seconds. They replied:

"Believe in the Lord Jesus, and you will be saved, you and your household."[9]

This is one of the most profound encounters in all of history. By responding that very hour, the jailer and his family received the free gift of God's grace.

Post-New Testament

The above simple, 14-word, five-second message has been repeated millions of millions of times in the past 2,000 years. It is so short and simple, many cannot accept it. Many stumble on it. It is not sophisticated or complicated enough. It is even too simple for many "religious" people, who are careful to add to it their own requirements. But, like the jailer, millions have accepted it and have received grace.

As examples, I can think of three young boys. At different times in their lives while growing up they had the opportunity to hear this "good message" of what God had done for them. In each case, in about one minute, they decided to believe the message and receive it into their hearts. God's grace was instantly given. The reality

Chapter 7: The World's Greatest Experience

of their experience has been confirmed many times. I know this is true; they are my sons. And this same experience has been seen in millions of families and individuals all over the world, in every nation and tongue.

You, too, can have this experience—in just one minute! When you do, you enter into "the world's greatest life," described next.

00:01:00

ONE MINUTE SUMMARY
The World's Greatest Experience

Like Abraham, you can "believe the Lord," and it will be "credited" to you as righteousness. Believe what He says about his Son ("believe" means to entrust yourself to Him) and be declared innocent.

Like Moses and the Israelites during Passover, you can, by faith, apply the blood of the Lamb of God, Jesus, to the doorposts of your heart. God will "pass over" you in dispensing justice and consider you "not guilty." God sees the blood and considers that punishment has already been taken by His Son in an act of substitution, for our sakes. However, if one rejects God's sacrifice, it denies Him a just (legal) basis for removal of guilt. It must remain.

Like the thief on the cross who acknowledged Jesus' identity and recognized his own dire need, you also can cry out, "Jesus, remember me." You, too, will join Him in Paradise the day you leave this earth.

About 800 B.C., the prophet Joel said that a time would come when "Everyone who calls upon the name of the LORD will be saved,"[10] (literally in Hebrew, "the name of 'Yahweh,'" God's actual name). *That time is now.* Yahweh has appeared in the flesh as salvation with the Hebrew name "Yehoshua" or "Yeshua," (meaning "Yahweh is salvation")—"Jesus" in English. You can call upon His name, and you will be saved. And now, a summary of the incredible and marvelous

One Minute (or less) Procedure: *Call upon the name of the Lord (Yeshua, or Jesus), and you will be saved*

Or Alternate Procedure: (Like the jail guard who wanted to know what he had to do, you can...) *Believe in the Lord Jesus, and you shall be saved.*

CHAPTER EIGHT

The World's Greatest Life

Chapter 8: The World's Greatest Life

There are two major consequences resulting from "the world's greatest experience" previously described:
1. A new and better life in this world, surely the world's greatest, and
2. An assurance and hope of a better life to come, also the greatest.

This chapter will address the first point—a new life in this world; the next chapter will address the second—the life to come.

This book is mostly about the new covenant, or eternal blood covenant. God initially spoke of it through the Hebrew prophets, then later implemented it. As quoted in the Letter to the Hebrews, the Holy Spirit said through the prophet Jeremiah:

"This is the covenant that I will make with them after those days, says the Lord: I will put my laws on their <u>hearts</u>, and write them on their <u>minds</u>."[1]

The old covenant under the (Old Testament) law was an external thing. All over the world today "religion," per se, is largely an adherence to an external set of rules, standards, and rituals. Unfortunately, even some Christian circles have not escaped the mindset that religion is "doing" (or not doing) something rather than "being" (although the "being" will always result in a "doing"— the former is causative). However, the *new covenant* was intended to be, and is, a unique and profound internal phenomenon.

The Old Testament law was described by Paul as a "custodian" until the Messiah came. The analogy has sometimes been used of a fence that restricts a child from going into the street to hurt himself. The fence only restricts; it doesn't change the desire of the child to go into the street. Ideally, the child's desire would be changed, making the fence unnecessary. The law would be "in the heart."

There was once a brilliant and intellectual atheistic teacher who delighted in attacking young Christian students. He tried to demolish them with his clever arguments. He knew all the answers,

Chapter 8: The World's Greatest Life

he thought. One day he was scheduled to counsel a young lady who was known to be unashamed of her faith. The teacher couldn't wait. He purposed to "put her in her place" and destroy her silly notions about this so-called Christ, especially the resurrection. They met, and the teacher skillfully berated her, trying to tear down everything she believed in. Finally, the young lady politely said, "But sir, I know that Jesus rose from the dead. I know that He's alive."

Surprised, the angry teacher exclaimed, "But how can you be so sure?"

With a sweet smile, she assuringly replied, "I just know it's true because He lives in my heart."

In a swift reversal, the teacher's own intellectual arguments were destroyed, and he was totally disarmed by the young lady's experiential testimony. He was not prepared for that; he had no argument. She communicated and radiated a reality that he could not explain. This is a true story. After this experience the Jewish teacher soon became a believer in the Messiah and later a powerful teacher of the Bible whose own life has impacted many.

The story is important because it demonstrates an important principle regarding this "new life." It is not just a new way of looking at things. It is not just a new orientation or philosophy. You may look the same in the mirror. You may sound the same. In many ways you may act the same (although there may be some notable exceptions!). But you are *not* the same, because, according to the Bible, you have a "new life."

You can't hear it, touch it, or see it, except its results. But it's there—in the spirit realm. You can't see gravity either, or love, or peace, but they are nevertheless real. You see the results of them. In God's eyes in the spirit realm, a transformation takes place. Jesus called this experience being "born again," although the phrase is misused and misunderstood today. Paul elaborated on the idea and said:

> *"If any one is in Christ, he is a new creation; the old has passed away, behold, the new has come."*[2]

Chapter 8: The World's Greatest Life

The New Life

What is this new life, and why is it so great? Is it just a retread of our old self? Hardly. Several years ago a selected group of famous theologians around the nation was asked to list what they thought were the greatest principles taught by Paul the apostle in his letters. They all listed several. Of course, "justification by faith" was agreed among them all. But so was another principle that is one of the least understood and appreciated among believers today—"union with Christ."

This is one of the most astounding and mind-boggling phenomenons described in the Bible. It is a repeated and persistent theme, and not just an isolated reference. Here is exactly what happens: at the moment that *grace* comes to you when you believe in Jesus and what He did, the Spirit of God Himself comes and takes *residence* in you, joining Himself with you and you to Him. *You become one.* It is an experiential happening. Not theoretical—real.

Prior to that event, your spirit was real, but "dead" spiritually, or void of God's own life. In such a condition one might even think that it is God, not oneself, that is dead. His is the only true life in the universe, a never-ending, positive life of love, joy and peace. When your spirit is joined with His, you, too, have that eternal life. You are in union with that life. He lives "inside" of you. The young lady in the previous story was referring to this when she said, "He (Jesus) lives in my heart."

> *"He who is united to the Lord becomes one spirit with him."*[3]

> *"Do you not know that your body is a temple of the Holy Spirit within you?"*[4]

> *"How great among the Gentiles are the riches of the glory of this mystery, which is <u>Christ in you</u>."*[5]

Remember Chapter 4 and the "inter-union" principle of the blood covenant? Our inter-union with God is a result of this covenant.

This is difficult to understand because it's mystical and spiritual. It does not conform to our physical frame of reference. But neither does God. What could be more mystical than thinking that a Supreme Being could create the universe out of nothing? Or what could be more mystical than thinking that the death of a person almost 2,000 years ago could affect your eternal destiny? So don't worry about the reality of spiritual principles. They are not only real; they are *more real* than physical principles. How? Because all visible matter is temporal, whereas spiritual reality and principles are eternal. That's why the Bible counsels us to let our minds be set on eternal things.

I Live; Yet Not I

When, by faith, grace comes to us, God so completely identifies with us that He considers us to have actually been on the cross with Jesus. Our "old self" literally died with Him and a "new self" rose with Him in the resurrection. In describing this wonderful paradox, Paul even exclaimed:

"I am crucified with Christ: nevertheless I live; yet not I, but Christ liveth in me."[6]

That's the way God looks at us. That's why He can look upon us as "perfect," even though it doesn't appear that we are. When He looks at us He sees our sins dealt with on the cross in His Son, and He sees the Son instead of our old self. And the more we can, by faith, see ourselves the same way God sees us, the more spiritual and eternal reality can break through and be manifested in this temporal existence.

Outside (Inside) Help

A tremendously practical application results from this. When one receives Christ, one really receives the Holy Spirit—that aspect of God's being that is manifest in the world today, coming after

Chapter 8: The World's Greatest Life

Christ ascended bodily into heaven. The Holy Spirit is described as the Comforter, Helper, Counselor, and Spirit of Truth (a "He" and not an "it")—the Spirit-person of God Himself. Before He departed, Jesus said:

> *"And I will pray the Father, and he will give you another Counselor, to be with you for ever, even the Spirit of Truth, whom the world cannot receive, because it neither sees him nor knows him."*[7]

The Holy Spirit does, in fact, help, comfort, counsel, guide, protect, illuminate, teach, and empower, to name a few of His activities. He is, really, the ever present and indwelling Christ.

Believers often discover the importance of the Holy Spirit the hard way. Our own zeal and energy can carry us but so far. We seem to run out of steam in trying to live the Christian life with our own efforts. We then learn a great truth: we literally cannot do it, and do it consistently. This experience teaches us that only the indwelling Christ can do it through us. We experientially learn of that great paradox mentioned above: "I...yet not I...but Christ."

We Are Not Alone

We are not alone. This is the profound truth of the Christian experience in this life. We are not just looking forward to the sweet bye-and-bye, but we begin to experience God Himself in this life. Upon entrusting oneself to Christ, one immediately obtains a constant companion and partner. Jesus said:

> *"I will never leave thee, nor forsake thee."*[8]

With this promise and reality God has provided an answer to one of the deepest and most pervasive problems of humanity—loneliness. People can be lonely even in a crowd of other people or when constantly surrounded by relatives and friends. It is a spiritual loneliness, a sense of isolation in the universe—an emptiness. It can be hell on earth, a little taste of what eternity would be like without God's presence. On one occasion when describing the coming of the Holy Spirit, Jesus said:

"He dwells with you, and will be *in you*."

The presence of the Holy Spirit helps us to overcome the trials, temptations, problems, and hurts of this life and this world. God's people are not immune to these things. Look what happened to Jesus Himself. And all but one of the original apostles were martyred for telling the "good news." But there's a big difference. God is with us to the end—helping, comforting, and encouraging. He didn't promise to spare us from all troubles, but to help us as we go through them.

Gifts and Fruit of the Spirit

The Holy Spirit's presence is not just an inward experience, but also an outward one. If we are, indeed, "dwelling places" for God's Spirit, does it not make sense that this "other Person" inside of us would like to express Himself? He surely would not like to remain mute. Actually, there are many things that God wants to do on the earth, and He has chosen to operate through people: to people through people. It is a cardinal principle that God will not usurp our wills. If He did so, we would merely be automotons and not the free moral agents He wanted in creation. Therefore, He expresses Himself through us as we allow Him. He desires to "reign" in our hearts and lives, but only with our permission.

This "other Person" in our lives is described as having incredible power—the power that formed the heavens and also raised Christ from the dead. It is the power of an infinite number of atomic explosions rolled into one. And the Bible reveals that as God indwells us, He wants His power to flow through us. Before Jesus ascended into heaven, He told His disciples:

"But you shall receive power when the Holy Spirit has come upon you."[10]

Chapter 8: The World's Greatest Life

The Greek word for power is *dunamis*, where we get the word for dynamite. The disciples did receive it, giving that original small group of believers and later others the ability to shake the world. People today pray for and receive that same Holy Spirit power, and they, too, shake the world around them for Christ. Scholars do not agree on whether all believers have that latent power which can be released by faith-inspired action, or whether it is a special endowment. But we do know for sure that it is real, and that "faith" is the channel of release. Power is only latent until it is released. Faith is the detonator. Also, many believers report "powerless" lives until they prayed and asked for the Spirit's empowering and equipping for service. Our finite minds cannot understand the process; we only know of its reality.

God's power is dynamite power, but yet it is a controlled power. The actual fruit, or some say "personality," of this Person's life in our lives is described as:

> "*love, joy, peace, patience, kindness, goodness, faithfulness, gentleness, and self-control.*"[11]

It seems strange but also logical that the Spirit-Creator wants to express His own life and actions on Planet Earth through its human inhabitants as He is allowed to indwell and guide them. And all of God's purposes are constructive, positive, and helpful in every aspect of human activity. At the end of human history, perhaps the saddest commentary will be that humanity "quenched" the activity of God's Spirit[12] and brought its problems upon itself.

We have talked about *faith*, and we have talked about *love*. There's one more element of the famous triad that remains. Mental health professionals declare that this other element is essential for human life. Without it we can die. That element is *hope*.

In the next chapter I want to tell you about "the world's greatest hope."

00:01:00

ONE MINUTE SUMMARY
The World's Greatest Life

The new life that results from believing in Jesus, the Son of God, and entrusting our lives to Him is not just a turning over of a new leaf or a new resolution to "do better." It is actually a totally new spirit life. The One Minute Experience actually "births" an eternal spiritual existence. It brings the human spirit truly to life for the very first time and joins the person in an actual "union" with God's own Spirit. While appearing physically the same in a mirror, the individual is now different at the core, at the spirit level and is a dwelling place of the Holy Spirit.

> *"He who is united to the Lord becomes one spirit with him... Your body is a temple of the Holy Spirit."*

By yielding to God's presence and guidance, the "new creation" person can actually allow the Creator's own life to be expressed in the world and thereby accomplish His purposes. This duality of existence, Creator and creature, is referred to in the Bible as both a mystery and a paradox. Nevertheless, it is real: two but one; one but two. "I live; yet not I, but Christ liveth in me," declares Paul. On the "I" or human side, we can still act selfishly, bringing temporal results and ultimate unhappiness. Or we can "yield" to God's presence and let Him have His way through us, manifesting His power and personality, bringing eternal results and happiness for both others and ourselves.

This latter option is a wonderful privilege. And without a doubt, it is "the world's greatest life!"

CHAPTER NINE

The World's Greatest Hope

Chapter 9: The World's Greatest Hope

It's fun to have something to look forward to, isn't it? It adds zest to our lives. Expectation makes it easier to get out of bed in the mornings. Something is ahead that we can anticipate doing or seeing, and it's exciting. It gives us an inner motivation to keep on going. We humans need something good to hope for and to anticipate.

No Hope

Without hope, some say, we can die. With nothing to live for there is just despair; the future is bleak, blank, and void of meaning. Some people tragically find themselves in this condition. With nothing to look forward to in this life or a life beyond, they reach their end. Some people go into depression; others anesthetize themselves with alchohol or drugs. Some try to lose themselves in certain activities. Some commit suicide. "Misery loves company," so some spread their misery to others by becoming philosophers of despair, expressing themselves in music, literature, and art. The world is full of it.

Those who reject God have a meaningless existence—really worse than an animal, which cannot contemplate its mortality—and a future completely void of any hope. Several years ago a famous movie star expressed this while on his deathbed. His loving daughter was at his bedside. His final tragic words to her were, "I'll never see you again." He had no hope.

A famous atheist spent a lifetime denouncing God. But on his deathbed, he was overcome with fear. He screamed in anguish at the thoughts of his imminent death and what was ahead for him, while at the same time cursing the God whose existence he had always denied. He had no hope.

A medical doctor's life was dramatically affected when a dying man, moments before his death, clutched the doctor and begged, "Save me. Oh, please save me. I don't want to go to hell." He then died, without hope.

Chapter 9: The World's Greatest Hope

The darkness of hell will have a total and pervasive sense of hopelessness. Ultimately, this will be a chief characteristic in an a Christless eternity. It will be the maximum horror. Some may scoff at hell's fire, but hopelessness will be a worse fate.

Hope in Christ

But in Christ, we have "the world's greatest hope." As we discussed in a previous chapter, it is not only for God's companionship and help in this life, but for the life beyond! God has promised an endless existence in Paradise with Himself to those who will accept His gift—free to us but purchased with His own blood.

> *"What no eye has seen, nor ear heard, nor the heart of man conceived, what God has prepared for those who love him."*[1]

We know very little about this future existence. Only limited information has been given. With our finite minds it is really impossible to imagine an infinite existence; thus, "nor the heart of man conceived..." But God has revealed some things about it. One thing we know is that Jesus is there in the glory of His deity, and we will see Him. While on the earth He prayed:

> *"Father, I desire that they (those who believe in him) also, whom thou hast given me, may be with me where I am, to behold my glory which thou hast given me in thy love for me before the foundation of the world."*[2]

Actually, he "went ahead" of us to prepare things for those who would put their trust in Him:

> *"In my Father's house are many mansions: if it were not so, I would have told you. I go to prepare a place for you...that where I am, there ye may be also."*[3]

What Is Prepared

We know that it will be a place where there is no sickness, pain, sorrow, or death. No cancer. No heart attacks. No AIDS. No aging. Perfect and permanent health and well-being. No hospitals. No (practicing) doctors.

Not a trace of defilement or corruption. No deception or misrepresentation (no television commercials!). No theft. No crime. Nothing but truthfulness and honesty. No (practicing) lawyers (some say none at all, but I know that can't be true).

No immorality. No wars. No conflict. No worry or anxiety. No taxes! No Internal Revenue Service (IRS agents? Maybe). No depressing newspapers or television network news. Nothing but good news.

A constant *joy*. A perfect *peace*. A pervasive *love*.

We will see departed loved ones who had placed their trust in Christ. There will be a grand and glorious reunion. What a happy experience to see each other again in an infinite existence! We will also meet people of history who lived before us, with us, and after us. What a thrill!

A famous basketball player, "Pistol Pete" Maravich, unexpectedly died of a heart attack at the age of 40. But not long before he died Pete had committed his life to Christ. He testified that he finally had peace, a peace he had never known before. Pete is with Jesus now. Someday we can meet Pete and, who knows, maybe play a little ball with him. I trust my skills will be somewhat better. But never like "Pistol Pete," one of the best ever.

There will be some sort of meaningful, enjoyable and fruitful activity.

The beauty will be unimaginable. Light will be from the brightness of God Himself; no sun or other light will be necessary. His being will radiate the light. There will be colors and sounds that are beyond the present ability of our senses to perceive, and music beyond the ability of a thousand Mozarts and Beethovens to compose. Plus, in the best imagery of human language, structures of precious stones and streets of pure gold, "transparent as glass," are described.

The Lamb's Book

Actually, who all will be there? The Book of Revelation, the last book of the entire Bible, tells us:

"Only those who are written in the Lamb's book of life."[4]

There's that word *Lamb* again. We started talking about the Lamb in Chapter 1 and can't get away from Him. He's in the first book of the Bible and the last.

The apostle John was given a vision of heaven. He described the Lamb's eyes as a flame of fire, His voice like the sound of many waters, His face like the sun shining in full strength, and on His head many diadems. *The Lamb is clad in a robe dipped in blood*, the blood of the eternal covenant. On this robe is a name inscribed, "King of kings and Lord of lords."[5]

John also heard singing to the Lamb:

"Worthy art thou to take the scroll and to open its seals, for thou wast slain and by thy blood didst ransom men for God from every tribe and tongue and people and nation, and hast made them a kingdom and priests to our God."[6]

Then John reported that he heard every creature saying:

"To him who sits upon the throne and to the Lamb be blessing and honor and glory and might for ever and ever."[7]

The Second Coming

A peaceful, eternal, and heavenly existence is the assurance and hope of every person who puts his trust in Jesus the Messiah, the Son of God. But there will be one generation of humans who

Chapter 9: The World's Greatest Hope

will experience a startling incident and see Jesus in person while on the earth! They will be alive when the Messiah makes his second appearance in power and majesty, unlike His first coming in humility. This is a theme of both the Old and New Testaments. The "Second Coming" of Christ is referred to approximately 1,845 times in the Bible, 318 times in the New Testament alone!

During the 40 days after His resurrection Jesus made many appearances to show Himself alive. He spoke His final words, then:

> *"When he had said this, as they were looking on, he was lifted up, and a cloud took him out of their sight. And while they were gazing into heaven as he went, behold, two men stood by them in white robes, and said, 'Men of Galilee, why do you stand looking into heaven? This Jesus, who was taken up from you into heaven, will come in the same way as you saw him going to heaven.'"*[8]

Jesus had previously spoken of this future event. It was to follow a time of great trouble on the earth and a regathering of the scattered people of Israel. He had prophesied the destruction of Jerusalem and the dispersion of the Jews around the world. The destruction occurred a few years later in the Jewish-Roman war of A.D. 66-70. Like the Old Testament prophets, He also spoke of a future return of the Jews to their homeland and the retaking of Jerusalem from "the Gentiles."

Now, after 2,000 years of nonexistence, the nation of Israel has been reestablished in our generation. The Middle East is a powderkeg of conflict caused mostly by a hatred of Israel, a Semitic family rivalry going back thousands of years. The industrialized world is lubricated by Middle East oil. One is reminded of something the Hebrew prophet Zechariah said nearly 500 years before Christ. He spoke of a time in history when Messiah would return and referred to the "house of David and the inhabitants of Jerusalem...when they look upon him whom they have pierced." Zechariah said:

Chapter 9: The World's Greatest Hope

> *"Thus says the Lord...Lo, I am about to make Jerusalem a cup of reeling to all the peoples round about...a heavy stone for all the peoples; all who lift it shall grievously hurt themselves. And all the nations of the earth will come together against it."*

We have seen hints of this already with the entire world economy teetering on the availability and price of Middle East oil and the potential for war. And most of the "nations of the earth" in the United Nations, led by the Soviet block and "nonaligned" nations, are vehemently anti-Israel. Is Zechariah's prophecy being fulfilled?

Are we near Christ's return? No one knows. It may be very, very soon. Or it may be another 2,000 years. But we are told to look for the signs. There are things we are told that will happen, after which:

> *"And then they will see the Son of man coming in a cloud with power and great glory. Now when these things (the signs) begin to take place, look up and raise your heads, because your redemption is drawing near."*[10]

Paul refers to this momentous event when he says:

> *"For this we declare to you by the word of the Lord, that we who are alive, who are left until the coming of the Lord, shall not precede those who have fallen asleep. For the Lord himself will descend from heaven with a cry of command, with the archangel's call, and with the sound of the trumpet of God. And the dead in Christ will rise first; then we who are alive, who are left, shall be caught up together with them in the clouds to meet the Lord in the air; and so we shall always be with the Lord. Therefore comfort one another with these words."*[11]

I just complied with Paul's instructions in the last sentence above. Be comforted...

Without question, we have the "world's greatest hope." There's just nothing like it. Someday we'll see Him, the one who formed

Chapter 9: The World's Greatest Hope

the universe and designed the worlds, the flowers, the amazing human body, and the one who chose to take on the frame of a humble servant, and to serve as a sacrificial Lamb. We will live with Him in an indescribable paradise for ever and ever, without end.

Paul referred to us as

> *"awaiting our blessed hope, the appearing of the glory of our great God and Savior Jesus Christ, who gave himself for us."* [12]

The hope we are awaiting is not fantasy. It is not just wishful thinking. It is as valid as God's own integrity and promises. It is an inevitable happening. *Yet, still a hope.*

> *"Now hope that is seen is not hope. For who hopes for what he sees? But if we hope for what we do not see, we wait for it with patience."* [13]

00:01:00

ONE MINUTE SUMMARY
The World's Greatest Hope

Hope is the essence of life. Without hope, life cannot exist, at least in any meaningful way, and sometimes not at all. The greatest horror is hopelessness. The greatest threat to any human is an endless existence of hopelessness, void of any chance to know or experience God. Hopelessness is surely the chief characteristic of a Christless eternity.

Conversely, the greatest hope possible for any human is that is given in Christ—to see Him and to dwell with Him forever in Paradise!

Total peace, total joy, and total love. Indescribable beauty. Indescribable sounds. No sickness, pain, sorrow, or death. No dishonesty, corruption, or crime. No taxes! No depressing daily newspapers or television network news.

There will be a joyful reunion with loved ones who trusted the Savior. We will meet people of history who lived before us or after us. Such an infinite existence is really beyond our finite imaginations, thus the description:

"What no eye has seen, nor ear heard, nor the heart of man conceived, what God has prepared for those who love him."

One generation of humans will be alive and see Jesus at the "Second Coming." This startling event is a major theme of both the Old and New Testaments.

All this—the return of Christ and an eternity of bliss—is not an empty or wistful hope, *but an inevitable happening*, yet still a hope.

"Now hope that is seen is not hope. For who hopes for what he sees? But if we hope for what we do not see, we wait for it with patience."

Chapter 9: The World's Greatest Hope

"we wait for it with patience."

CHAPTER TEN

The World's Greatest Privilege

Chapter 10: The World's Greatest Privilege

Have you ever tried to talk to the mayor of your city by telephone? Or get a personal appointment? It would be difficult, maybe impossible in a large city.

What about the governor of your state? Can you imagine how difficult it would be to make an appointment with the governor to unhurriedly discuss things that are personally important to you?

Or consider the President of the United States. It would be virtually impossible. You would not even get through to the secretary. Forget it.

The above people are humans, just like us. They put on their clothes, brush their teeth, and do everything else just like any other person. Even if you could see them, you would have to make an appointment, usually far in advance. And when you found yourself actually in their presence, you would probably experience a feeling of awe and privilege. That's because they are important people. They have a lot of authority. But just human authority, of course.

Now compare their importance and authority with that of the Creator of the universe, the King of kings and Lord of lords—the One who is enthroned in the heavens and sovereign over all creation. It's really silly to even compare.

But the absolutely amazing thing is that you can meet with and converse with this King at any moment of any day, for any length of time, about any subject. You don't have to go through a secretary. You don't even need an appointment. In a sense, you can really just "barge right in" any old time—respectfully, of course. Actually, He's delighted to hear from us, so much so that He's always ready.

This act of conversation with the Creator is called *prayer*.

Too often prayer is regarded as a ritualistic burden only to be endured. Anything can be turned into a dreary ritual if we allow it. But like other spiritual truths and realities, in the proper perspective they can be natural, normal, and exciting. Prayer, for

Chapter 10: The World's Greatest Privilege

example, when viewed in the above light becomes an act of awe, wonder, and privilege. It is really "the world's greatest privilege."

Why Pray

Prayer is important for several reasons.

1. Prayer pleases God. A praying creature recognizes his Creator, who desires a relationship. A relationship without communication is not much of a relationship. Also, proper prayer exalts God with praise and worship for who He is.

2. Prayer keeps us in communication with the One who sustains our life. Actually, His own life and thoughts flow from Him to us as we commune. Failure to pray can block the flow.

3. Prayer allows God to speak to us, and to guide and use us for His purposes.

4. An often overlooked truth is that even though God is sovereignly powerful, He has chosen to let His activities and involvements in human affairs be governed in large part by the prayers of His people. He has a "will" in all matters, but He desires that His people cause that will to be implemented by prayer. This amazing principle allows a divine/human partnership with eternal results. Only a loving God would conceive of such a plan. In itself, this is the world's greatest privilege. Such prayer, as aided by the Spirit of God Himself, may be directed toward any subject: nations, leaders, family, friends, self, or any person or situation.

Item 4 needs some clarification. God is not a cosmic errand boy, just waiting for His orders. The principle is much deeper. Only God's will is ever going to be done through our prayers regardless of what we pray. And our prayers will be more effective if we understand His Word, obey Him, and remain in tune with His will. But the profound principle here involves one of God's chief attributes described in an earlier chapter—justice. Both justice and love govern God's actions; they also govern prayer.

With humanity, God has established a race of creatures with a free will. He has purposed not to interfere with that free will.

Chapter 10: The World's Greatest Privilege

But when we pray, we "permit" or justify (give lawful permission to) God to act in a situation where He previously allowed His hands to be tied. We freely choose to invite His intervention. It justifies Him to act if we pray according to His own will. With prayer, both justice and love are served according to the divine plan.

How to Pray

I am not going to give you a lengthy methodology. Many books have been written on this subject. The Bible contains many examples, principles, and exhortations. I want to keep it simple. I want to just give you the basics. This book is not intended to be inclusive or give you everything—just to get you started, or help you along.

There is one principle requirement for entering into God's presence with prayer, a requirement that God revealed through the Hebrew people and that has never changed. The discussion of the ark of the covenant in Chapter 4 addressed this principle. Also see Appendix II. In early Hebrew history, God's presence was within the Holy of Holies within the tabernacle, or temple. He could only be approached by the high priest who entered to sprinkle blood on the Mercy Seat. There was no other access to God. The high priest represented all the people. Any of the people's individual prayers throughout the year were made possible by this periodic blood atonement. It gave them access to God Almighty.

This practice ceased in the first century. It ceased because Messiah came as a final and lasting sacrifice for all people everywhere. He is called the "great high priest." It is His own blood that now provides our access to God.

In the old Hebrew tabernacle and temple, there was a *curtain* hanging in front of the Holy of Holies, blocking access to the Mercy Seat. Several strange things happened at the very moment Jesus died on the cross. There was an earthquake. Hugh rocks were split in two. Tombs opened and dead people arose and appeared to many. The sun stopped shining. But also,

Chapter 10: The World's Greatest Privilege

> *"the curtain of the temple was torn in two, from top to bottom."*[1]

This supernatural occurrence signified that the old way had ceased and that now the Son had provided access to God through His own blood. There is now no more curtain. No more Holy of Holies. No more blood on the Mercy Seat. No more temple. But there is a way. Yeshua (Jesus) said:

> *"I am the way... no one comes to the Father, but by me."*[2]

This is why Jesus repeatedly exhorted us to pray and ask "in my name." His name is the only one that has credibility. It is the only one that attracts attention in heaven. It represents the only one who paid the price for the access and privilege—the price was His own blood.

You can chant mantras and incantations for a month. You can fast for forty days. You can stand on your head. You can invoke anyone's name. But if you do not come in the name of the One whose blood provided the access, you cannot enter the Holy of Holies in the heavenlies and come before God's presence, because it is the blood that makes it possible. Remember the chasm we described in Chapter 6? There is just no way across the great chasm separating God and humanity except the way God Himself has provided.

God's way is the way of mercy. It springs from His own great love and sacrifice. If anyone proclaims another way, such an act ignores what God has done and contemptuously spurns the blood of the eternal covenant; plus, it says that God's sacrifice was unnecessary. But in reality, any other way is delusion and futile.

Secular mentality says that such a way is too narrow. Anyone with that view will have to take up the matter with the One who devised it. But it's certainly not narrow—it took centuries of prophetic announcements and orchestration. Also, the way is open to anyone, without exception.

Step One, then, is to come before God with *faith* in the Son and His atoning blood sacrifice. Prayer itself and using His name express that faith.

The Bible reveals that without faith it is not possible to please God, and also that He rewards those who diligently seek Him.[3] Prayer is both an exercise of faith and of seeking. We know from the Bible that prayer pleases Him, and that if we are diligent, He will reward us.

Other Prayer Principles

Where to pray? Anywhere. Regardless, in the privacy or "closet" of your heart.

When to pray? Any time.

Eyes closed or open? Either.

Physical position? Any.

How? For our part, vocalization is scriptural. There is something mystically real about a vocal declaration and profession. But surely, an inward meditation is also heard. On God's part, He speaks to us in our spirit, usually gently and in a way that comforts and brings peace and assurance. If we have disobeyed Him, it may be more like a rebuke; but if we are repentant, He is quick to forgive and restore. A major way to judge whether we are hearing God's voice is to check it against His Word, the Bible. God will not contradict Himself.

Subject or object of prayer? Focus on God and His being. Speak praise and worship. Remember thanksgiving and gratitude. Mention specific needs of yours and others as they come to your mind. Review "the Lord's Prayer" given by Jesus (Matthew 6:9-13) for His guidance on content and priorities.

Heavenly Review

Someday in heaven I just know God is going to ask many of us, "Why didn't you talk to Me more? There was so much I wanted to do for you and say to you. Remember those problems you were having about...? But you wouldn't talk to Me or listen to Me very much. I set up such an easy system for everyone; it's hard to believe more people didn't take full advantage of it."

Chapter 10: The World's Greatest Privilege

We'll have a lot of excuses. Some may say they were too busy. "Well, Lord, I was pretty busy, you know—meetings, television, and stuff like that." He may choose to show us the cost of our earthly prioritization, what might have otherwise happened. Others may say, "Frankly, Lord, I just didn't feel worthy enough. I figured that people who prayed a lot had to really feel worthy." He'll remind us that it was His blood that makes us worthy and absolutely nothing that we do, nor is it affected by how we "feel."

"It's not what you did. It's what I did for you! You would have known that if you had studied My Word," He may say. "At least you should have learned that from Bramlett's book that I sent you."

00:01:00

ONE MINUTE SUMMARY
The World's Greatest Privilege

He's easier to contact than the mayor of your city, the governor of your state, and certainly the President of the United States. No appointment necessary. No need to go through a secretary. He's always available, 24 hours a day, and for any length of time, on any subject.

The person? None other than the Creator of the universe—the King of kings and Lord of lords. Such access (prayer) is undoubtedly "the world's greatest privilege." Prayer (communication) is important for our relationship with our Creator. It opens the channel for His thoughts to guide and comfort us. Further, God has chosen to place limits on His activity on earth based on the prayers of His people. That is because He has chosen not to interfere with our free wills. Our prayers "permit" or justify God to act in human affairs. By His own principle, if we pray according to His will we release Him to act in a situation, making us co-laborers in eternity. There is one principle requirement for access to God. It was first revealed to the Hebrew people and was a strict Jewish practice for hundreds of years: access was only available through the blood atonement. Access is still available only through the blood atonement, but the Old Testament sacrifices ceased in the first century. They ceased because the Messiah came and provided that blood atonement and access to the Father for all people everywhere.

We can pray anywhere, anytime, in any position, for any duration, on any subject. Prayer should include praise, worship, thanksgiving, and requests. Prayer is an exercise of faith. Such prayer pleases God and brings results.

CHAPTER ELEVEN

The World's Greatest Obligation

Chapter 11: The World's Greatest Obligation

Does it all sound too easy so far? You may be wondering, "Where's the gimmick?" Well, no gimmick. But God's gift of grace must be taken very seriously. It imposes on us an obligation even greater than one's duty to nation, family, or anything else.

In return for His "free" grace, what does God want from us? Could it be just an hour or so one day a week. Or at least attending a service on Easter, just to make Him feel better? Or maybe a few dollars in an offering plate occasionally? These are popular misconceptions. Actually, God doesn't "need" our attendence anywhere, any of our money, or really anything. He is totally self-sufficient, and He owns the universe.

But He does *want* something from us, something far more substantive than the above. *He wants our lives!*

Sound scary? Does it sound like another one of those good news - bad news situations? Well, maybe at first glance, but it's really all good news. The only reason He wants our lives is so that He can give us His life in return! Remember, God is totally selfless, loving, and giving. Anything He wants from us is really designed for our ultimate good. He has even devised the ultimate gift—Himself! This gift was first manifested at the crucifixion ("For God so loved...that He gave...") with a *general* gift for all humanity. Now it is the gift of His own Spirit, His very life, to each *specific* person individually.

Chapter 8 described this new life that is implanted within us. This chapter will discuss some of the practical applications of that wonderful principle and how our wills (which we still have) and actions should respond to God's love, allowing His *implanted* life to *supplant* our own.

Since Jesus was on the earth almost 2,000 years ago, church leaders, theologians, and other thinkers have contemplated and debated the relative importance and interrelationship of two great principles:

Chapter 11: The World's Greatest Obligation

1. God's *free gift* of grace

versus

2. Humanity's *required response*.

Some seem to get overemphasize and get out of balance on one, and some on the other. Too much emphasis on God's grace invites license and irresponsibility, one group says. Another group says that putting too much emphasis on man's response dishonors God and exalts man's ability. Yet both are valid. God's grace is a free gift, but yes, there is a required human response.

However, there does seem to be a general agreement (and confirmed by my own study and experience) that because God is so great and we are so relatively weak, He must even give us the *enablement* to respond properly. His Spirit must prompt us to recognize what He did in Christ. He must help us see the need for repentance and forgiveness. He must help us overcome temptation. He must help us to love other people. He must help us do whatever He wants us to do. As we learned in Chapter 8, the Holy Spirit is called the "Helper."

Yet we must respond, even with that help. But He is there to help us with a nudge, with encouragement, with the strength that we need. We do it together. Jesus and I. Jesus and you. Because of that we can respond. We do respond. Ultimately, our wills act, but that action springs from an enlightened mind and heart. We are motivated to respond because:

1. Love begets love. Once we grasp the love of God and what He has done for us through the blood covenant, we are compelled to respond in kind. We desire to show our deep gratitude and to please Him.

> *"The love of Christ controls us...he died for all, that those who live might live no longer for themselves but for him who for their sake died and was raised."*[1]

2. In spite of this love, we are still mindful of God's holiness and power. We are instructed to live "with reverence and awe."[2]

Chapter 11: The World's Greatest Obligation

The apostle Paul reminds us of both "the kindness and the severity of God"[3] — immeasurable kindness towards humanity, yet the severity of a loving Father when correction is needed.

Discipleship

The above verse mentions no longer living for ourselves but for Him. Jesus made some rather hard and sobering statements about the cost of discipleship:

> *"Whoever does not bear his own cross and come after me...(and) does not renounce all that he has cannot be my disciple."*[4]

The word *disciple*, which comes from the same root as *discipline*, means a pupil, or adherent. To become a disciple means to commit oneself to follow Jesus. To "renounce" does not necessarily mean to arbitrarily dispose of possessions, but primarily to renounce them as a priority, as their pull may interfere with commitment. Some who follow Jesus today, such as those in communist countries and cultures with religious repression, face persecution and death constantly because of their faith. In America and other nations with religious freedom, we have not been called to that sacrifice. But we should be willing if necessary, nor should we balk at smaller sacrifices such as service within our church and the sharing of our time and resources as may be needed by others.

Can one be a party to the blood covenant and be anything less than a 100% committed, all-out disciple, renouncing everything? Scholars debate this. My own view is that since the blood covenant is a faith-produced contract, it stands alone as a tribute to God's grace. The Bible is clear, however, that faith will always result in some corresponding action. But what percentage of our activity qualifies us to be called a disciple? Has any human truly reached 100%? Not to my knowledge. In God's perspective, it must be a matter of the heart attitude. Sometimes we fail, but God looks upon the heart.

Chapter 11: The World's Greatest Obligation

This is dangerous ground. Our weakness must not be viewed as a cop-out. We are all undoubtedly capable of deeper degrees of commitment and response to God's love and call. The Bible also reveals that there will be eternal rewards based on our response, though that should not be our motivation.

The world and popular opinion warn us against becoming "fanatics." Face it, you will be considered an oddball if you make a sincere effort to follow Jesus. Of course, you will be considered quite normal if you freak out following a drug-using rock music star, or if you commit your life to most any other cause.

People do, indeed, decide to sacrifice everything for all manner of temporal causes. Consider the British explorer early in the century who advertised for men to accompany him on an expedition to the South Pole. His ad read:

> "Men wanted for hazardous journey. Small wages, bitter cold, long months of complete darkness, constant danger. Safe return doubtful."

One would doubt that there would be any response at all. But surprisingly, men signed up from all over England, willing to sacrifice for what they viewed as a worthy cause. Compare that cause with serving the Creator who sacrificed Himself for our sakes. And our commitment can have eternal consequences.

Or consider the young American college student who had been converted to communism. Billy Graham read a letter (condensed) from the student to his fiance, explaining why he had to break the engagement:

> "We communists have a high casualty rate. We live in virtual poverty, and turn back every penny we make above what is absolutely necessary to keep us alive. We communists don't have the time or the money for movies, concerts, or T-bone steaks or decent homes or new cars. I am in dead earnest. It is my life, my business, my religion, my sweetheart, my wife, my mistress, my bread and meat. I work at it in the daytime and dream of it at night. Its

hold on me grows, not lessens, as time goes by. Therefore, I cannot carry on a friendship, a love affair, or even a conversation without relating it to this force which both drives and guides my life. I've already been in jail because of my ideas and if necessary I am ready to go before a firing squad."

The late Vince Lombardi was one of the greatest football coaches and motivators who ever lived. He demanded total, fanatical commitment from a group of adult and educated men—commitment to simply a game to move a leather bag full of air (a football) up and down a grassy field. But he also related it to life:

"The many hurts seem a small price to pay for having won, and there's no reason at all, which is adequate, for having lost. To the winner there is 100% elation, 100% laughter, 100% fun...And it is a game, I think, that is a great deal like life in that it demands a man's personal commitment be toward excellence, and be toward victory...it must be pursued with all of one's might...And I want to say that the quality of any man's life has got to be a full measure of that man's personal commitment to excellence and to victory regardless of what field he may be in."

In view of humanity's proven ability for commitment to all manner of worthy and unworthy causes, is our Creator's request for commitment to Himself unreasonable? As to priorities, could there be any higher?

What God Wants From Us

As a creature aware of a loving and all-powerful Creator, we cry out, "What does He want me to do?" Just the question is pleasing to God, because it speaks of our desire and willingness. And just the sincere question assures that the answer will be forthcoming.

One day a group of people asked Jesus the question: "What must we do, to be doing the works of God?"

Chapter 11: The World's Greatest Obligation

Jesus replied:

> *"This is the work of God, that you believe in him who he has sent."*[5]

In His reply, Jesus stressed the priority of *faith* before *action*. As described earlier, the word "believe" connotes the idea of trust and commitment. No human effort has eternal value outside of that which has been entrusted to and enabled by God Himself.

This is Step One: believing and entrusting oneself to Christ. This act alone not only triggers the gift of grace and eternal life but it is the precondition for accomplishing anything for God or anything with eternal value.

So we do that. Then what are we supposed to do? The Bible is full of laws, do's and don't's. The Old Testament has elaborate systems of laws on dozens of subjects and, of course, the Ten Commandments. Many were for a specific purpose in Hebrew history. Many were prophetic. Many contained eternal principles that are reiterated in the New Testament. However, we learn from the New Testament that Jesus fulfilled those old laws, that they all found embodiment and satisfaction in Him. The New Testament gives us a more brief and simpler rule, although the old moral principles remain in force:

> *"This is his commandment, that we should <u>believe</u> in the name of his Son Jesus Christ and <u>love</u> one another."*[6]

Paul reiterates our Step Two:

> *"He who loves his neighbor has fulfilled the law. The commandments, 'You shall not commit adultery, You shall not kill, You shall not steal, You shall not covet,' and any other commandment, are summed up in this sentence, 'You shall love your neighbor as yourself.' Love does no wrong to a neighbor; therefore love is the fulfilling of the law."*[7]

That is the summary of our obligation. It does not cancel the old moral commandments mentioned, but rather explains their basis in a broader sense.

Sound too easy? Just "love." Well, if you haven't discovered it yet, you will—it's the toughest assignment on earth: placing the interest of others above our own, *always*. Complicating the process is the difficulty in always knowing what is best for others; we just don't always know. Love is not always "giving in." And try as hard as we may, we sometimes find ourselves failing even on the obvious things. No one has ever perfectly complied with the love commandment except Jesus Himself. This keeps us humble and constantly relying on God's grace and not our own abilities.

We are also dependent upon His guidance and wisdom as we constantly face decisions regarding relationships with others which are too unique or specific to be found in a written code of law. Remember? The old covenant was simply keeping "external" rules; the new covenant involves God's internal guidance in keeping with the "spirit" of the law in all situations. (Those who are still trying to live under the old written law have a codified system of centuries of interpretations and opinions trying to cover every situation, which few have even read, much less understand or comply with.)

Actually, there are many forms the above "love law" can take. The New Testament exhorts us about many things we should do and things we should avoid in order for our lives to be effective instruments for God. For example, we are instructed to help others, to be patient and kind, to pray, to bless and not curse our enemies, and avoid immorality, idolatry, jealousy, enmity, drunkenness, and other "works of the flesh," as they are called.

We are not addressing here vocational service or specific full-time callings. A full discussion of how to determine a "calling" and God's will in vocational matters, including chapters of practical job-hunting guidance, is contained in my book, *Finding Work*, (Zondervan Publishing House).

The Church

One activity that God has ordained and blessed for our participation in serving Him is the church. We are encouraged not

Chapter 11: The World's Greatest Obligation

to neglect "to meet together, as is the habit of some, but encouraging one another..."[8]

God is corporate-minded. He sees us not only in union with Himself but also with other believers, all functioning together in a mystical body that He inhabits and through which He operates. It is in the church that we find teaching, care, counsel, and the operation of spiritual gifts (talents, abilities, "manifestations of the Spirit") for the "common good." It is also the place where we can worship jointly, serve and be channels of these blessings for others. The functioning community of believers is very important and has high priority in the Scriptures.

There are mystical but very real and practical reasons for the church's importance. Jesus said that whatever we do to others we do to Him. Somehow, as we relate to others, we relate to Him. He also promised a special presence whenever multiple believers get together in His name, and a special power when believers agree together for prayer needs. Also, as with any group or purpose, there is a synergistic effect involved in unity (the whole is greater than the sum of its parts). Finally, unexplainable and positive "happenstances" occur as believers interrelate—blessings from God through members of His Body.

You may be able to commune with God by yourself at home, in the woods, or while playing golf, and you should, but doing this as a substitute for church is not God's plan or instruction as He has very specifically revealed.

But how does one pick a church? It can appear confusing because there are so many churches and denominations and varieties of doctrine. How does one avoid getting involved with the "wrong kind," such as a cult? It is both a difficult and an easy question.

First, pray and ask God to lead you. Leading you is His job. He will. Second, recognize that no single church or group has a monopoly on all the truth. Different denominations and groups seem to emphasize different aspects of God's truths. Rather than isolated pictures, together they are like a mosaic of the larger and beautiful pattern of Christ's Body on earth. The most important thing is that their emphasis is on the One who referred to Himself as the embodiment of all truth—Jesus Christ.

Chapter 11: The World's Greatest Obligation

Regardless of denomination, affiliation, or name, make sure that the particular church in which you may be interested has these essential ingredients:

1. Preeminence is given to Jesus Christ, His deity, His atoning blood sacrifice, and His actual presence in the church. All matters within the church, even the organization, should be subordinate to this cardinal truth, not just in word but in deed.
2. Belief that salvation is "by grace through faith," and not by human works, law-keeping, or church-related activity.
3. Belief in the Bible as the inspired Word of God.

There are individual churches in every historic denomination and many independent groups that meet the above criteria, and some that do not; name is no guarantee. A warning sign may be a persistent obsession with contemporary social/political issues popular with the media at the time (not to be confused with genuine social concern), rather than proclaiming God's spiritual truths.

Beware of False Cults

Besides the usual churches one might encounter, there are many cults and false religions that have the trappings of Christianity but are deceptively and dangerously different. They even existed in the first century. Paul warned:

"Fierce wolves will come in among you, not sparing the flock."[9]

Here are some ways to test for a cult or heretical group. Use the three criteria above, plus one or more of the following may apply:

1. A cult will sometimes have its own book, in addition to the Bible, which it considers inspired. It will typically conflict with but be given priority over the Bible. Lacking knowledge of the Bible's truths can make one a vulnerable candidate for any cult.

Chapter 11: The World's Greatest Obligation

2. Cults often center around one strong leader or founder who is typically autocratic, if still alive, or abnormally revered if not alive.

3. A cult or its leader or founder will often have the only "true" interpretation of Scripture, usually involving a particular doctrine around which the cult organizes and makes itself different from others.

4. Cults will typically ignore Bible truths that may contradict their tenets, or will take particular Bible truths and distort and overemphasize them beyond God's intent.

5. A cult is often "exclusive," considering outsiders as unsaved and not recognizing other believers in Christ as part of God's family.

6. Cults tend to impose a bondage of allegiance, instilling the fear that leaving their group will cause a loss of salvation.

7. Some modern cults are an offshoot of Eastern religions, teaching nonbiblical concepts such as reincarnation, Eastern meditation, and a "Christ spirit" or "universal spirit" within everyone. It is a play on semantics. They are not talking about the same Christ. Modern cultism also includes so-called "New Age" groups that are flourishing that are actually "occult" in nature—stressing spiritism and psychic phenomenon. These offer counterfeit spirituality, and a horrible danger—missing the real thing.

8. Cults will often force servitude to their group or leader, perhaps as "evidence" of one's sincerity or salvation, whereas Christ wants us to voluntarily serve Him out of a right motivation.

Christians have an obligation to God, as previously discussed. However, there is still a wonderful freedom in Christ and in a believer's walk in the Holy Spirit. It is not a freedom to sin, but a freedom to serve Him out of a heart of love and without the bondages that humans often impose on one another.

> *"You, my brothers, were called to be free. But do not use your freedom to indulge the sinful nature; rather, serve one another in love."*[10]

00:01:00

ONE MINUTE SUMMARY
The World's Greatest Obligation

God's free gift of grace *versus* our required response—a source of theological debate for centuries. Both are true, but the emphasis is on the former, because we need the help of God's Spirit, the "Helper," even in our responses. Yet we still must respond. We respond (1) in appreciation for the love He has shown for us, and also (2) out of reverence and awe of who He is.

What does God want from us? What does He want us to do? The New Testament summarizes it this way: "believing" in the Son of God (entrusting ourselves to Him), and "loving one another."

The "entrusting" involves commitment and discipleship, radically changing our former priorities and, if necessary, being willing to sacrifice or suffer for Christ's sake. The "loving" involves placing the interests of others before ourselves, which summarizes all of the Old Testament law.

In our own human strength, both the above are impossible. We must constantly rely upon God's Spirit for assistance, and His grace when we fail.

The New Testament exhorts us to do many things to make us more effective instruments for God. This includes helping others, kindness, praying, giving, and serving. It also exhorts us to avoid certain things such as idolatry, immorality, enmity, and covetousness.

A major obligation is for believers to assemble together for joint worship, fellowship, teaching, and mutual service. God has ordained the church for this purpose. Believers should prayerfully pick a church that is Christ-centered and honors the Bible as God's Word, and carefully avoid the many false cults.

Chapter 11: The World's Greatest Obligation

"This is his commandment, that we should believe in the name of his Son...and love one another."

CHAPTER TWELVE

The World's Greatest Conflict

Chapter 12: The World's Greatest Conflict

This chapter I would prefer to leave out, but I must include it for the sake of completeness and candor.

If you have responded to the One Minute Procedure, you have entered a war, a literal war. It's every bit as real as an actual military war, and more difficult:

"He who rules his spirit (is mightier) than he who takes a city."[1]

Ruling our own spirit is really "the world's greatest conflict." It is a two-dimensional conflict.

Conflict With Our "Flesh"

First, our new spirit life, joined with the Holy Spirit, comes in conflict with the fleshly, or human nature side of ourselves. Peter spoke about:

"The passions of the flesh that wage war against your soul."[2]

These passions are not limited to sexual desires. If expressed according to God's plan, sexual desires are not evil in themselves; they were given by God to propagate humanity. The word "passions" has a broader meaning. The "flesh" represents our whole sensory being and the physical world's constant pull against us: things we see, hear, feel or otherwise experience in the world of appearances that may be contrary to spirit-reality and God's will. It includes the constant temptation toward *selfish* actions instead of *selfless* actions in accordance with the law of love. Paul said:

"The desires of the flesh are against the Spirit, and the desires of the Spirit are against the flesh; for these are opposed to each other, to prevent you from doing what you would."[3]

Paul even confessed his own struggle in this area, but he also gave us the solution. He told us that even though our old human nature may appear to be alive and may try to assert itself, in God's eternal perspective the old nature is, in fact, dead, having been buried with Christ. Our practical application of this spirit-truth is, by faith, to "consider" it so, and then act like it. Actually, that's how all spirit-reality is made to penetrate the sensory world—by *faith inspired action.*

> "So you must also consider yourselves dead to sin and alive to God in Christ Jesus."[4]

At one point, Paul described his personal battle. He cried out in desperation, then followed with the solution:

> "Wretched man that I am! Who will deliver me from this body of death? Thanks be to God through Jesus Christ our Lord!"[5]

Conflict With Evil Spirits

The conflict above is primarily an internal one. The second conflict is from external sources, although the battle is still fought internally. This is the conflict with the devil and his angels, called demons. They are invisible, but very real spirit-beings. They are not omnipotent as God is and have been given only limited domain, primarily through the wills of people who "allow" them, though perhaps unknowingly. We will not explore the full scope of the operation of these rebellious angels who were banished from heaven except to mention that they are a source of part of our battle. On this Paul said:

> "For we are not contending against flesh and blood, but...against the spiritual hosts of wickedness in the heavenly places."[6]

What are the symptoms of a life that is in the heat of spiritual warfare and under attack by Satan? They can be many and varied. Satan usually plays upon our weak points, which will vary with individuals. He operates in the realm of the mind, suggesting and tempting, but where it seems like our own thoughts. Satan need never be successful in his attacks, but where he is experiencing success symptoms might include coldness toward things of God and an unusual attraction toward things contrary to spiritual health. They may include obsessive and detrimental behavior. Symptoms often include a great sense of discouragement, anxiety, hopelessness, fear about the future, or depression (fear is the opposite of faith; depression the opposite of hope). It should be remembered, however, that demonic influence or attack does not necessarily mean "possession" in the sense of ownership. Satan can only claim and possess those who have rejected God. In fact, a possessed person really has no interest in pleasing God. If you are concerned about yourself and you want to please God, you cannot be possessed. You only need to appropriate your victory in the present battle.

Prescription for Victory

Paul then prescribes the solution to the warfare, a spiritual "armor" that will allow us to win in this inevitable struggle. He tells us to be "strong in the Lord and in the strength of *His* might," clothing ourselves with God's provisions for victory, such as truth, peace and faith (see Ephesians 6:10-18).

Such a struggle may seem like bad news. One might say, "Why bother? Who needs all of that?" Well, it's really good news. You see, if you do not enter the battle, you actually surrender without a fight. You have already lost and are captive to both your sensory self and the spiritual forces of darkness in the universe. That is not a viable alternative. Also, it is only through a "battle" that a "victory" can be obtained. We have been called to battle, and most importantly, to victory.

In the last book of the Bible, the Book of Revelation, Jesus gives some wonderful promises to those who "overcome" and who

Chapter 12: The World's Greatest Conflict

obtain victory. He knows how tough it is. Remember, He walked this way. And He has purposed to help us. There is a simple remedy, described by the apostle John:

> "This is the victory that overcomes the world, our faith."[7]

The faith referred to is faith in God and His blood sacrifice which, through our confession, mysteriously renders Satan powerless and defeated. This idea is repeated in another verse which speaks of the believers' victory over Satan:

> "And they have conquered him by the blood of the Lamb and by the word of their testimony, for they loved not their lives even unto death."[8]

In his majestic and beautiful hymn, "A Mighty Fortress is Our God," written over 400 years ago, Martin Luther translates this remedy into a simple method of defeating Satan:

> "The prince of darkness grim
> We tremble not for him;
> His rage we can endure,
> For lo! his doom is sure,
> One little word shall fell him."

Our inner faith, which itself is a gift from God, and our words and actions that spring forth from that faith, give us sure victory over self and Satan in the greatest of all conflicts.

00:01:00

ONE MINUTE SUMMARY
The World's Greatest Conflict

Each individual, who through a spiritual rebirth has been joined to Christ, is now engaged in a war. It is a war against (1) the natural, human nature that is subject to the passions of the material and sensory world pulling one toward self-gratification and away from serving God and others, and (2) actual spirit-beings who inhabit the world of darkness and who, while perhaps giving up on capturing our souls for eternity, try to discourage us and nullify our effectiveness for God.

There is no avoidance of this conflict. Those who reject God's great sacrifice have capitulated and, whether they realize it or not, are already captives of their natural self and the spiritual forces in conflict with God. Believers in Christ have the privilege of battle—and victory!

God has many wonderful promises for those who overcome. Plus, he has given us the means: His presence and help, and the gift of faith.

"This is the victory that overcomes the world, our faith."

And remember all of our previous discussion about the Passover Lamb and His blood? The last book of the Bible speaks of our overcoming and, apparently in retrospect, speaks of how we secured victory over Satan and the things that would otherwise destroy us:

"And they have conquered him by the blood of the Lamb and by the word of their testimony, for they loved not their lives even unto death."

APPENDIX ONE

The World's Greatest Questions

Appendix 1: The World's Greatest Questions

INDEX

Can the existence of God be proven? 166

What is God like? 166

Where did God come from? 167

How do you explain the "Trinity?" 167

Does evil really exist, or is it just relative? 168

Why does a loving God allow so much evil? 169

But what about happenings that are no one's fault? 169

Are all religions just different paths to the same God? 170

What about those who have never heard the gospel? 171

Is reincarnation possible? 172

Can life after death be proven? 173

Is there a literal hell? 173

Can we know the future? 174

Are we near the end of the world? 175

Which is the best, or "one true church?" 176

Why do Christians sometimes sin? 177

Appendix 1: The World's Greatest Questions

THE WORLD'S GREATEST QUESTIONS with One Minute Answers

The following are among the greatest and most frequently asked questions in the world, questions that people ask others or maybe just ask themselves. The answers provided can be read within approximately one minute.

QUESTION: *Can the existence of God be proven?*

ANSWER: The Bible does not attempt to "prove" the existence of God; it simply declares Him to be. The very first verse of the Bible says, "In the beginning God..." The Bible also declares that every human has an innate awareness of His existence and that His reality is seen in creation.[1] God is spirit and thus infinite; His being cannot be subjected to physical laws, nor to human experimental methods. However, philosophers have put forth powerful and logical arguments for God's existence, such as the Cosmological Argument (there must be a "first cause"), Teleological Argument (the intelligent "design" of the universe reveals a "Designer"), Ontological Argument (that a finite being can even conceptualize an infinite Creator is evidence of His existence), and several others. Individually, each argument is extremely persuasive, but collectively they are so overwhelming that they put the entire "burden of proof" on the other side of the question—to prove that He does *not* exist in the face of all the evidence! Perhaps the greatest proof we have (other than observed creation) is the birth, life, death, and resurrection of Jesus Christ. In addition are the objective and subjective effects of His life and ministry. The psalmist, King David, said, "The fool says in his heart, 'There is no God.'"[2] Everybody else knows that there is.

QUESTION: *What is God like?*

ANSWER: The Bible reveals many attributes of the personality and character of God. Like a person, He has person-ality and char-acter. He is eternal, a spirit-being. He is omniscient (all-knowing);

Appendix 1: The World's Greatest Questions

nothing escapes His knowledge. He is omnipotent (all-powerful). He is omnipresent (everywhere present). He is all-wise. As a being, God apparently also has emotions. We are told that He grieves, and also laughs. He is holy, pure, righteous, and perfect. He is also revealed as faithful, merciful, kind, and loving. In fact, He personifies love so much that the Bible declares, "God is love."[3] He is also just and intolerant of sin and evil. But in His love, He has provided an answer to these things through His Son. In Jesus the fullness of God was said to dwell, so if we want to know what God is like, we look at what Jesus is like. "He who has seen me has seen the Father," Jesus said.[4]

QUESTION: *Where did God come from?*

ANSWER: Time is a human frame of reference, always dependent upon the movement of matter, such as the earth around the sun, moon around the earth, hands around a clock, or human activity. God exists outside of this frame of reference, in eternity, where there is no beginning or end as we think of it. His actual name as He revealed it to Moses in the Hebrew language is YHWH, or "Yahweh" (mistakingly called "Jehovah"), a derivative of the Hebrew word, "to be." He also referred to Himself as the "I am," in Hebrew meaning a self-existent, self-causing, eternal being. Yahweh is the first cause of all causes and effects. Jesus referred to Himself as that same "I am" of the Old Testament who has always existed. Since He used Hebrew terminology reserved for deity, the religious authorities of His day thought Jesus was blaspheming. God was not created, or else there would be another God. He was, and is, and always will be.

QUESTION: *How do you explain the "Trinity?"*

ANSWER: As the ancient Hebrew Scriptures say, "Hear, O Israel: the LORD our God is one LORD."[5] Both Jews and Christians know that there is only one God, and not three. Yet there is a mysterious plurality of His nature that the finite mind cannot understand. In the Hebrew Scriptures the noun used for God (Elohim) is a plural noun. Also, in the above quote the word *one* is from the Hebrew word *echad*, sometimes meaning a "composite oneness" or "diversity of unity" rather than the absolute number "one." At the beginning of creation God said to Himself, "Let *us* make man in *our* image."[6] In the New Testament, in speaking of the Father, Jesus said, "I and the Father are one."[7] Much is also said about the Holy Spirit, the Spirit of God. Though we may not be able to understand this tri-unity, we know that God is Father, Son, and Holy Spirit—three manifestations of the one and same God for different times and purposes. Many human analogies attempt to explain this, but they are all inadequate. It has been said that the Father is God invisible, the Son is God manifested, and the Spirit is God in interraction with His creation.

QUESTION: *Does evil really exist, or is it just relative?*

ANSWER: One cannot view human history or our current world without concluding the reality and absoluteness of evil. Extremes include Hitler's death camps, the genocide in Cambodia, rapes, murders, and drug distribution. On a smaller scale, there is the constant stream of deception and corruption in governments, businesses, and in individuals. Organized crime has infiltrated industry, unions, and government itself. Evil literally pervades society, more than we often realize, affecting most everything we do. If we are honest, we even see it in ourselves. We may say or do something that will hurt someone else, sometimes even those who love us the most. Or evil may manifest itself by our omission rather than commission—not doing something we should do, instead of doing something we shouldn't. Only the Bible addresses and explains the mystery of evil, and gives its solution. Humanity's propensity for evil traces back to the very first humans. It is always related to self-seeking: the use of one's free will to exalt or advance oneself at the expense of others. Evil is also personified in a spirit-being named Satan, an angel who tried to exalt himself in heaven and usurp God, resulting in his expulsion. Satan has been given limited authority on earth. In the realm of the spirit and through the mind and personality, Satan operates through people. Sometimes he merely influences a person's behavior. But if they have rejected God, he possesses them. A person can reject God in their lives to the point where they actually relinquish their wills to Satan; whether they even believe in Satan's reality is irrelevant.

QUESTION: *Why does a loving God allow so much evil?*

ANSWER: The answer is implicit in the question: He "allows" it. He doesn't cause it. As mentioned earlier, evil is the result of volitional creatures, creatures with a free will who can make choices. God's alternative was to make puppets or automatons instead of people. But God wanted creatures made in His own image—spirit beings who could "choose" to love Him. His purpose was an eternal love relationship. He desires to share His entire Kingdom with cognizant creatures:

> *"that in the coming ages he might show the immeasureable riches of his grace in kindness toward us."*[8]

Thus, love motivated the creation of a humanity with the potential to do evil. Then, when evil was committed, love motivated a solution by which to restore humanity back to the relationship for which it was created. Evil and sin grieve God, and He longs for us to turn toward Himself and be forgiven and reconciled. (See "message of reconciliation"—Chapter 6.)

QUESTION: *But what about disasters and accidents that are no one's fault?*

ANSWER: Accidents are often traced to human sin, such as drunken driving or wanton carelessness, acts that can hurt ourselves and others. However, injury, sickness, and death do occur from things seemingly apart from any human cause, such as earthquakes, tornadoes, natural disasters, and some diseases that seem beyond our control (why are natural disasters always called "acts of God" but He is rarely given credit for the good things?). We do know that God has established physical laws that work consistently, such as gravity. Biological laws control our bodies as well as germs and

Appendix 1: The World's Greatest Questions

viruses. Sometimes, however, a higher spiritual law such as prayer may override them. We cannot always understand why certain things happen, but we do know from the Bible that a sparrow cannot fall to the ground without God's knowledge. How much more is He aware of and concerned with human activities? On one occasion, Jesus was asked a question similar to this. His answer was that God has a purpose even in disasters. An amazing attribute of God is that He can take an evil and convert it to a good purpose. Also, we tend to look at things from a temporal, short-term perspective, whereas God sees the much more important eternal consequences. Our walk in this life is by faith in an all-wise and all-loving Father who cares for us greatly and who is sovereignly in control of His universe. There is no such thing as "luck" or "accident." Whatever happens, we can be assured that for God's people it is a blessing, though sometimes in disguise. This reality is a source of peace. Those who reject God are faced with the horror of being subject to the constant threats of a seemingly capricious, impersonal, and dangerous world.

QUESTION: *Are all religions just different paths to the same God?*

ANSWER: There is a great myth about "religions." Christianity is not really a religion, but a "relationship" with God through His Son. Jesus claimed exclusivity—to be *the* Way, not *a* way. He also claimed to be God in the flesh. No "religion-founder" ever claimed that. Actually, most of the others never intended to start a religion. This includes Confucious and Lao Tzu whose later followers combined their teachings with superstitions, deifying the founders who would probably denounce such an act if still alive. Hinduism has no founder and has about 330 million gods. Its chief one, Brahman, is not really a god at all but an "it." The founder of Buddhism, Siddhartha Gautama, was influenced by Hinduism. He kept some of it and rejected some of it. Buddhism is primarily an ethical system. Gautama never claimed to be divine or even to have divine revelation. The Buddhism religion is not a path to God, but to Nirvana. But Buddhists cannot agree what it is, except a void or nothingness. Islam's Qur'an (Koran), which contains the writings

Appendix 1: The World's Greatest Questions

of Mohammed who was born over 500 years after Christ, is in serious conflict with the biblical revelation, a unified work that spans 40 generations and was authored by 40 different people. For example, the god of Islam is impersonal and without love or mercy, just the opposite of the truth. In Islam, Mohammed is considered the greatest prophet, and greater than Christ, who was just another prophet. With Judaism, God "chose" the Hebrew people through whom to reveal Himself, His commandments, and His plan of redemption for the entire human race. However, much of modern Judaism has no similarity to the ancient faith but is more a cultural or ethnic identity, based largely on collective rabbinic traditions. The Hebraic revelation was completed in one particular Jew, Yeshua (Jesus) the Messiah, who fulfilled the Hebrew prophecies. Only in the Bible is God revealed to us as a personal and loving Father, who Himself solved man's sin problem by His own great sacrifice. Only He gives us hope with a wonderful plan for the future. This is the "good message" or gospel.

QUESTION: *What about those who have never heard the gospel?*

ANSWER: Most people would be astounded if they knew how pervasively among the nations and cultures the gospel has been communicated over the past 1,900 years. In some remote areas of the earth there is more love for Jesus than we see in America. Yet, it is true, many have not heard. That should motivate us all the more to fulfill the Great Commission of Christ: "Go into all the world and proclaim this good news." The good news not only gives hope of life after death, but it sets people's spirits free from fear and superstition in this life. Some entire cultures are economically and politically depraved due to spiritual darkness, with people living in fear of demonic idols and dying of starvation while "sacred cows" roam the streets. God wants them to know of His love and provision for them. But will God allow an eternal hell for those who do not hear? We only know what has been revealed to us. Beyond that, we do not know all of God's plan. The Bible says that all humans instinctively know of God's reality. There is evidence that people will be judged on the light they have been

Appendix 1: The World's Greatest Questions

given, and what they do with it. Other than that, we will just have to trust in God's fairness, of which we can be assured. We also know for sure that:

> *"God gave us eternal life, and this life is in his Son.*

QUESTION: *Is reincarnation possible?*

ANSWER: The idea that people's souls can migrate back to the earth as other people or as lower life forms has its roots in Hinduism and its concept of *karma*, or the law of moral consequence. According to karma, what a person is in this life depends on what he did in a previous life. One goes through a virtually endless cycle of rebirths to reach a final state of bliss, unlikely because perfection must be achieved to get there. An "unrighteous" life, however, may result in the next life as an insect or other creature (although Western concepts of reincarnation do not include lower life forms). A major problem is that it's not clear what the "rules" for righteousness are. It's a "Catch 22" situation (uncertain rules, but whatever they are you can't keep them perfectly anyhow, but you must keep them to reach perfection—or else!). This is a demonic theology of hopelessness and void of love that has millions living in fear and total superstition in a belief system that equates a cow with God. Millions of people are also locked into a "caste system" of extreme depravity caused by their presumed deeds in a previous life. A Hindu verse says, "Worship, O Cow, to thy tail hair, and to thy hooves...The Cow is Heaven, the Cow is Earth, the Cow is Vishnu (God), the Lord of Life."[10] The Bible says that:

> *"It is appointed for men to die once, and after that comes judgment."*[11]

The Bible also declares that *no one can make himself righteous or worthy*. With a free gift, God has settled that problem once and for all in His Son, whose own righteousness is "credited" to us when we put our trust in Him. At the above mentioned judgment, we are seen as clothed in the righteousness of this One who became our substitute.

> *"We have been sanctified through the offering of the body of Jesus Christ once for all.*[12]

We don't have to wander through endless lifetimes in a futile self-effort of trying to reach perfection. God has already solved our problem. And we can appropriate His solution in just One Minute! Incredibly good news!

There is evidence that demonic spirit-beings sometimes operate through human personalities. These spirits may have operated through humans in other generations, making it appear that the present human habitation has experienced things in a past life. That is the probable explanation of alleged recall from the personalities of people from the past. This may also be the answer to so-called "multiple-personalities" that psychiatrists can only label but not explain.

QUESTION: *Can life after death be proven?*

ANSWER: Jesus proved it. There is much empirical evidence on both the reliability of the Scriptures and the resurrection of Jesus Christ. It is not in any way a blind faith in an unsubstantiated historical claim. See Chapters 1 and 2. The New Testament talks a lot about the next life. Paul said:

> *"If Christ has not been raised, your faith is futile and you are still in your sins...If for this life only we have hoped in Christ, we are of all men most to be pitied. But in fact Christ has been raised from the dead...For as by a man came death, by a man has come also the resurrection of the dead. For as in Adam all die, so also in Christ shall all be made alive."*[13]

QUESTION: *Is there a literal hell?*

Appendix 1: The World's Greatest Questions

ANSWER: Yes, in the sense that there is a literal place or existence in eternity for those who have willingly rejected God. It was never created for people, but for angelic beings who had experienced God's glorious presence and who, in spite of their experience, rebelled against Him in heaven. God does not send people there. They choose to go there by willfully deciding that they do not want God in their lives; *they obtain their own desire*. They discover too late that any blessings they had in this life were gifts from God and not from their own efforts or any human agency. Hell is a place without God, a place of remorse, hopelessness, darkness, and loneliness. No way out, forever. We don't know a lot about it except that it is a place to avoid at all costs. It is not a myth; Jesus spoke of it frequently. However, it is not known whether some of the language referring to it is literal or metaphorical. Jesus used the term, *Gehenna*, which was the name given to a refuse dump that burned constantly outside the city of Jerusalem. Whatever it is, absolutely nothing could be a worse fate. Sadly, it will contain people who did "good deeds" but thought they didn't need God in general, or the sacrifice of His Son, in particular. Interestingly, there will be "no hope" in either heaven or hell. In heaven, that which was hoped for becomes forever realized; in hell, forever deprived. The idea that lost souls cease to exist at death (the "annihilation theory") is contrary to Jesus' specific teachings, but is popular among some cults.

QUESTION: *Can we know the future?*

ANSWER: The Bible reveals much about the future in the writings of the only group of people in history with an infallible track record of prediction—the Hebrew prophets. Their record confirms the divine origin of their information. But the Bible also reveals that God desires individuals to walk by faith and trust in Himself. Detailed knowledge of the future would negate faith. Also, humanly speaking, a certain future is not inevitable, although God knows the outcome. Humans actually create and can alter the future with their wills, actions, and prayers. The New Testament speaks of "prophecy" as a valid gift and ministry even in our day. However, prophecy in the New Testament generally means speaking forth a message from God

Appendix 1: The World's Greatest Questions

and is not necessarily predictive. Such messages always relate to God's purposes as contrasted with the often silly and sensational "predictions" of popular psychics. Modern practices of astrology, fortunetelling, divination, psychic predictions, sorcery, and similar occult phenomenon are strongly forbidden by God (e.g., Deuteronomy 18: 9-14, Galatians 5:20, etc.). A large percentage of the practitioners are proven frauds, but biblically we know that some are in touch with "familiar spirits" (a scriptural term for demonic spirit-beings). Many occultists try to appear "religious," displaying the Bible, the symbol of the cross, pictures of Christ, statues, and similar trappings. Revelations from such practitioners are flawed, but can contain enough facts to deceive and trap a victim into "believing." As we previously discussed, "believing" is not a matter to be taken lightly. It produces commitment. We tend to become what we believe. The danger is that such practices can cause, at best, delusion, self-fulfilling mindsets and actions, fear, anxiety, and a lack of reliance on God; at worst, strong demonic influence in a victim's life, sometimes causing neurosis, psychosis, depression, and death. Anyone so involved should immediately stop, then pray, renouncing the involvement and asking God's forgiveness, cleansing, and deliverance from demonic influence. God tells us that if we acknowledge Him, trust Him with all of our hearts, and not depend on our own understanding, He will direct the path of our lives.[14] And we know that His paths are always paths of blessing and peace. I recommended reading: *Understanding the Occult*, by Josh McDowell and Don Stewart, published by Here's Life Publishers, Inc., San Bernardino, CA.

QUESTION: *Are we near the end of the world?*

ANSWER: The Bible does refer to a "new heaven and a new earth,"[15] and a time when the "earth and the works that are upon it will be burned up."[16] But even without the Bible, we know that someday our sun, which is only a medium-sized star, will burn out. Some astronomers believe it can last millions of more years, but others believe that about half of its hydrogen supply is depleted, causing it to be in danger of experiencing a "nova." A nova occurs when

Appendix 1: The World's Greatest Questions

a star gets brighter and hotter, then gets darker. Unfortunately, the U. S. President, Congress or probably even the United Nations would be helpless to do anything about it. Isaiah the prophet spoke of a time when "the light of the sun will be sevenfold."[17] The prophet Joel spoke of a time when "the sun shall be turned to darkness."[18] Jesus Himself spoke of a great tribulation on the earth just before He returns when "the sun will be darkened...and the powers of the heavens will be shaken."[19] We do not know when these things will be. Also, there is sincere disagreement among scholars on the order of events regarding Christ's return as well as its immediate effect on the world as we now know it. However, there are many "signs" given in the Bible for this momentous event. While some of these signs have appeared at various times throughout history, many scholars believe that this is the first time in human history that all the signs are converging. When speaking of His return, Jesus described these accompanying signs and said, "When you see all these things, you know that he is near, at the very gates."[20]

QUESTION: *Which is the best or "one true Church?"*

ANSWER: See Chapter 11 for guidelines on finding a church. All who put their trust in Christ are part of his spiritual body, a mystical union which transcends human organization and titles. In addition, there are many kinds of "local" churches or assemblies where believers meet for worship and service. Some are independent and autonomous such as the Baptists; others have a hierarchy of organization such as the Presbyterians. A friend once testified humorously how, when he was young, he had discovered the one true church. "It's where my mother goes," he said. "My mother wouldn't go to the wrong church!" A funny statement but often a true perception. Some groups claim exclusivity as the "one true church," but most now admit that the fabric of God's family is diverse in the practice of its faith. There is no compromise on the common denominators of all true Christian churches: the absolute deity of Jesus Christ, faith in Him as a prerequisite to salvation, and the Bible as the inspired Word of God. Beyond that there are many variations. The Bible should be the only guide to faith and

Appendix 1: The World's Greatest Questions

practice—all Christian beliefs and practices must be measured and judged by the Word of God. This may raise questions about the practices of some churches, but if they are not critically important doctrinal issues, confronting them may be more a source of discord than edification, which always must be our aim. No group has a monopoly on the truth. This is all demonstrative of the human condition that we all share. This gives us all the more cause to be grateful for God's mercy and to love and appreciate all who sincerely claim and proclaim Christ, the Son of God, regardless of affiliation.

QUESTION: *Why do Christians sometimes sin?*

ANSWER: People who do not want God in their lives often try to justify themselves by referring to Christians and saying, "I don't want to be associated with those hypocrites." Sadly, they are pridefully comparing themselves to other humans and rejecting an openness to God's only plan of mercy for themselves. This is a horrible price for pride and self-justification, really only a cover for rejecting God. And it will be an empty plea on Judgment Day. It's true, however, that Christians do make mistakes. But that only reinforces their need for God's grace as provided by the blood covenant. A bumper sticker says it well: "Christians aren't perfect, just forgiven." No one is more aware of his sinful nature than a sincere Christian trying to be obedient to his Master. Even for believers, the Bible talks about "the passions of the flesh that war against your soul."[21] These passions are every kind of selfish pull contrary to God's will, such as anger, enmity, lust, and covetousness. We are exhorted, with God's help, to be continuous overcomers. The Lord even taught us to pray, "Lead us not into temptation." But even though we are to aim for it, few if any reputable Bible scholars believe that a completely sinless state is possible in this life, something achieved only by Jesus Himself. So, occasionally one may slip. Unfortunately, we then discover that our mistakes not only hurt ourselves but other people, too. Sometimes we even bring discredit upon Christ through the image we project. Sin always hurts God, others, and ourselves. Any act of sin should bring a

Appendix 1: The World's Greatest Questions

believer to a remorseful confession to God. This triggers one of the most glorious and wonderful of God's promises:

> *"If we confess our sins, he is faithful and just, and will forgive our sins and cleanse us from all unrighteousness."*[22]

What is it that cleanses us from our sins? Remember Chapter 4 and the cleansing action of "the world's greatest substance?" In the same passage as above, we are told that:

> *"The blood of Jesus his Son cleanses us from all sin."*[23]

That is *the blood of the eternal covenant*, the very basis of this book, our lives, and all our hope.

APPENDIX TWO

The World's Most Mysterious

Disappearance

APPENDIX 2

The World's Most Mysterious Disappearance Solved in *One Minute!*

Chapter 4 referred to the famous *ark of the covenant*, the subject of the popular fictitious movie, "Raiders of the Lost Ark." A truth of the movie is that there really was an ark and that it really was lost! The fate of this ark is "the world's most mysterious disappearance." That is because there has never been a man-made object or artifact that has been as revered as the ark of the covenant. God Himself gave it special protection. Then all of a sudden—whoosh—it was lost in history.

Or was it? I believe I have discovered the location of the ark and why it has never been found! In fact, I am convinced. You will be amazed at the answer. You may even get to see it someday!

The Background

The ark was a wooden chest 3.75' long, 2.25' wide, and 2.25' high. God directed Moses to construct it in about 1491 B.C. Its purpose was to contain the two stone tablets of the Ten Commandments. It had a golden lid called the Mercy Seat (Hebrew for "cover"). It was placed in the Holy of Holies of the Tabernacle where God manifested His special presence.[1] Only the high priest could enter this awesome place. The high priest entered with sacrificial blood to sprinkle on the Mercy Seat. He represented all the people outside who depended on this procedure to remove the guilt of their sins. There is profound and prophetic significance to this and why God would only reveal Himself above the Mercy Seat, or "cover."

Appendix 2: The World's Most Mysterious Disappearance

As described in Chapter 4, the tablets of the Ten Commandments (the law) within the ark were constantly before God's presence testifying to the guilt of all the people. They represented God's holiness and perfect standard of behavior. But the blood sprinkled on the Mercy Seat "covered" and negated these accusations, even before reaching God. This blood "covering" was another prophetic symbol of the true *Lamb*, the Messiah, who was to come in the future and shed His own blood to "cover" the sins of all people everywhere. When applied, Messiah's blood covers and cancels the accusations of the law against a person. The law is eternal, and its accusations are correct and true against every human who ever lived. No one has ever complied with it perfectly; however, the blood covering invalidates the charges by shielding them from God. Because of the blood, He never even hears the accusations. It is as though they don't even exist.

Such an action is not arbitrary or without logic and rationale. The blood covering shows that the penalty has already been paid. The penalty for violating God's law is death, the Bible says. The blood covering represents that death. The Messiah Yeshua (Jesus) paid that penalty for every human by His substitutionary sacrifice for our sakes. Jesus is the eternal high priest who entered the Holy of Holies of heaven representing all people of all nations. He placed His own blood on the Mercy Seat before God as our "covering." His blood silences the accusations of the law against us. We become forever "not guilty."

The above is included to demonstrate the awesome importance and significance of the ark of the covenant. It was treated with the utmost fear and respect. On one occasion an unauthorized person touched it when he was not supposed to, then fell dead. God required his life. It was so holy that absolutely no mistakes were to be made regarding its handling and use.

Well, what happened to the ark? It was used by the Israelites for hundreds of years and suddenly it was no longer mentioned in history. Scholars believe that it was lost when the Babylonians captured Jerusalem in 586 B.C. But what was its fate? Was it destroyed, or was it kept and hidden by its captors? Because it was so holy, would God actually allow its desecration? Because it

Appendix 2: The World's Most Mysterious Disappearance

was so revered, it is very strange that no one, not even a Jewish writer, mentioned it again. And, of course, it has never been found by archaeologists. It has been a great mystery for about 2,500 years.

I believe that I have discovered the actual present location of the famous ark! In fact, there is not a doubt in my mind as to where the ark is at this moment. It is cared for, specially preserved, and in absolutely perfect condition.

00:01:00

The One Minute Solution

Here's the answer...

I have evidence that the ark and its contents—the tablets of the original Ten Commandments given to Moses by God—are actually located in heaven! How did it get there? I believe that the ark was literally "taken up" into heaven the same way that Enoch[3] and later Elijah were taken up.[4]

This is not just a personal opinion. I discovered it in the Bible, the Word of God. I was shocked when I found this, but it's very clear. The Book of Revelation tells us:

> *"Then God's temple in heaven was opened, and the ark of his covenant was seen within his temple."*[5]

Unquestionably, that is where it is. That's why it has been considered "lost" and why it is such a mystery. No wonder it hasn't been found. It wasn't meant to be found.

I once shared this discovery with a friend who had an advanced degree in biblical studies. He replied, "But I always thought that verse was metaphorical and not literal."

I said, "Well, maybe, but I'll tell you what. Let's just see. I'll bet you that when you get to heaven you will find the ark there just like it says." He didn't have an answer or take the bet. Of course, I was joking about a bet, but it made my point. I have

Appendix 2: The World's Most Mysterious Disappearance

no reason to suspect that the description is not literal. I believe that is exactly where the ark is at this moment.

Why would God take the ark and its contents directly to heaven? Well, no one knows. But I have a good idea. First, I believe it is because the ark and its contents, the tablets of the Ten Commandments, are so sacred. But more importantly, I believe it is God's plan for the presence of the ark to be an eternal testimony for the citizens of heaven—a testimony of the eternal blood covenant. It will be a reminder that He gave His own blood to "cover" the accusations of the law against His people. Not a bad reminder.

I hope it is there, for whatever reason. I want to see it. Then I want to say, "Thanks, Lord, for what you did for us. It's really great to be here."

See you there! Really, I'm counting on seeing you, whoever you are.

Look for me. I'll be the one with the big grin. And, hopefully, a basketball.

Be sure and tell me you read the book.

Appendix 2: The World's Most Mysterious Disappearance

"Now may the God of peace who brought again from the dead our Lord Jesus, the great shepherd of the sheep, by the blood of the eternal covenant, equip you with everything good that you may do his will, working in you that which is pleasing in his sight, through Jesus Christ; to whom be glory for ever and ever. Amen."[6]

Epilogue

A few parting thoughts...

1. Have you wondered why God instituted the One Minute Procedure whereby truth can be so simply communicated, received, and acted upon? I have. At first, it may not seem logical, especially to those who are gifted in their intellect, education, or physical abilities, and pride themselves on challenge and achievement. This may include many who are reading this book. Well, I have discovered the answer, and it is infinitely logical. Sometimes we forget that the range of human intellect and ability varies greatly. Your own ability may allow you to grasp the depths of theological truth or accomplish great things for the Lord, but many people in the world have limited intellects and physical abilities. A vast number of the people of the world have little or no education and cannot even read or write their own language. Many people are retarded, or infirmed, and handicapped. Some people just can't do anything. *Therefore, any fair and universal method for obtaining God's favor and grace must totally exclude any human activity*! (True Christianity is the only belief system which recognizes this. Virtually all Christian cults and nonChristian religions place primary emphasis on human activity—that favor from the Creator must be earned.) And in His infinite wisdom and love, God has given a method which is nondiscriminatory and is a common denominator regardless of intellect, education, age, economic status or physical condition—*faith*. Faith transcends all boundaries. Anyone can approach God with it, and on equal terms with all other humans. Only God could have devised such an ingenious method! Even a little child can do it, and sometimes more easily. Unfortunately, the simplicity of God's method is often a stumbling block for sophisticated people who pridefully want to interject their superior abilities and involve their egos. But Jesus warned, "Truly, I say to you, whoever does not receive the Kingdom of God like a child shall not enter it." [1] True faith will always produce some corresponding action, or evidence, in a person's life, but it's the faith that is key.

Epilogue

2. Belief is a decision. We discussed in a previous chapter how the word "believing" from the Greek carries the meaning of *entrusting* and *committing*. Thus, those who truly "believe" in Jesus, the Christ (Messiah), actually entrust their lives to Him. It's more than just an intellectual acceptance. For example, believing that a parachute will work is only an intellectual exercise until you decide to really entrust your life to it by jumping out of an airplane. The parachute saves you. You make a decision to really believe—to entrust. You literally throw yourself on the trustworthiness of the parachute. The same with christ. You throw your life on Him. You jump out of your former life and into Him. He saves you. The objective evidence of Jesus' messianic claim is overwhelming. To ignore or reject this fact, one has to make a conscious decision in the face of all the evidence. Or one makes a decision to believe. It's purely a volitional matter, and one for which we accept the consequences. Such a decision should not be based on emotion, although emotion may be involved. It is a conscious, rational decision to believe or not to believe based on the evidence. Of course, we know from the Bible that it is the Holy Spirit who helps and reveals, but when His job is done, a human decision still must be made. That decision has eternal consequences.

3. Probably the most profound question in the world is: "What is truth?" Everyone seems to disagree on everything: politics, economics, religion, psychology, and every other subject. We live in a world full of disagreement. And just when a person thinks he has discovered a fact, a theory, or a strategy he can believe in, he later finds it was flawed. It really never was the truth. As science makes new discoveries, even so-called physical laws that were thought immutable are found to have been in error. Recent discoveries show that even the most basic physical laws exhibit unexplainable patterns. How much more illusive is truth concerning nonmaterial reality? Does truth really exist? What is truth? That is the question the Roman governor, Pontius Pilate, asked Jesus just before Pilate sentenced Him to death.[2] Ironically, Pilate was looking truth in the eyes and did not recognize it, or Him. He was face to face with truth and could not see Him. Many are that way even in our day. This book is about "the world's greatest truths,"

Epilogue

but it's really about just one Person. According to the Bible, truth is not an abstraction. Truth is a Person. Jesus said, "I am the truth."[3] I hope you have found Him in the preceding pages.

It's been fun sharing Truth with you.

May He bless you richly....

NOTES

Scripture references are to the Revised Standard Version of the Bible unless otherwise indicated. References to the King James Version are indicated with KJV, the New International Version with NIV, and the Phillip's Modern English version by J. B. Phillips with JBP.

Prologue
1. Proverbs 8:10

Introduction
1. Trish Hall, New York Times News Service, quoted by *The Virginian-Pilot*, Norfolk, VA, January 2, 1988, page 1.
2. Hymn, *Amazing Grace*, by John Newton, 1779.

Chapter 1
1. Galatians 6:7
2. Ezekiel 26:3-21
3. Isaiah 66:8
4. W. A. Criswell, *Why I Preach That the Bible Is Literally True*, (Nashville, TN, Broadman Press, 1969), page 45.
5. Luke 24:25
6. John 14:26
7. For information on the works of Dr. Ivan Panin, contact Bible Numerics, 7600 Jubilee Drive, Niagara Falls, Ontario, Canada, L2G 7J6, telephone (416) 358-3000.
8. Jerry Lucas and Dale Washburn, *Theomatics*, (New York: Stein and Day, 1977).
9. George W. Cornell, Associated Press wire, quoted in *The Virginian-Pilot*, Norfolk, VA, August 16, 1986 (source of information on "Elohim" and "Torah").
10. II Timothy 3:16 NIV
11. Maybe the best and most exhaustive source and collection of facts relating to the reliability of the Bible is "Evidence That Demands a Verdict," by Josh McDowell, Here's Life Publishers, Inc., San Bernardino, CA, 1979.
12. John 6:63

Chapter 2
1. *One Solitary Life*, author unknown.
2. Luke 24:27
3. John 8:58 (He referred to Himself as "I am," as He did in Exodus 3:14).
4. John 14:9
5. Matthew 9:6

Notes

6. Matthew 5:21-48
7. Mark 8:31
8. John 20:28
9. Luke 21:27
10. Matthew 25:31-46
11. John 3:16
12. John 14:6
13. John 2,11; Matthew 8,14, and many others.
14. I Corinthians 15:6
15. C. S. Lewis, *Mere Christianity*, (New York: The MacMillan Company, 1952), page 45.
16. Frank Mead, *The Encyclopedia of Religious Quotations*, (Westwood: Fleming H. Revell, n.d.).
17. John 14:6
18. Ephesians 1:9-10 JBP
19. Editorial, *The Virginian-Pilot,* Norfolk, VA. Date unavailable.
20. Peter Marshall and David Manuel, *The Light and the Glory* (Old Tappan, N.J. Fleming H. Revell Company, 1977), page 31.
21. Phyllis Mackall, *God's Plantation*, research paper, unpublished, quoting from "A True and Sincere Declaration of the Purpose and Ends of the Plantation Begun in Virginia, 1610, the Virginia Company."
22. C. Gregg Singer, *A Theological Interpretation of American History* (Phillipsburg, N.J: Presbyterian and Reformed Publishing Company, 1964), page 45.
23. Marshall Foster and Mary-Elaine Swanson, *The American Covenant, the Untold Story* (Thousand Oaks, CA: The Foundation for Christian Self-Government), page 13.
24. Ibid., page 99-100.
25. Ibid., Page 69

Chapter 3

1. Romans 16:25-26
2. I Peter 1:10-12
3. Isaiah 7:14 KJV
4. Isaiah 9:6 KJV
5. Isaiah 53:3,5,7,10 KJV
6. Fulton J. Sheen, *Life of Christ* (New York, NY: McGraw-Hill Book Company, Inc., 1958), pages 11-15.
7. John 1:35
8. John 3:16

Chapter 4

1. Josephus, *The Jewish War* (New York: Dorset Press, 1959), page 372.
2. A classic work on this subject is *The Blood Covenant*, by H. Clay Trumbull,

a late 19th Century book. A copy can be obtained from Impact Books, Inc., 133 West Jefferson, Kirkwood, MO 63122.
3. Romans 3:2
4. Leviticus 17:11
5. Revelation 1:5 KJV
6. I John 1:7
7. Dr. Paul Brand and Philip Yancey, *In His Image*, (Grand Rapids, MI: Zondervan Publishing House, 1984).
8. Genesis 17:2
9. Genesis 17:9-14
10. Hebrews 9:15-18
11. Matthew 26:26
12. For detailed and fascinating explanations of symbolisms of the Messiah in the Passover traditions, the following books are recommended: *The Miracle of the Scarlet Thread*, by Richard Booker, Bridge Publishing Company, South Plainfield, NJ, 1981, and *Christ in the Passover*, by Ceil and Moishe Rosen, Moody Press, Chicago, 1978.
13. Matthew 26:27-28
14. I Corinthians 11:25
15. John 6:53-54
16. Genesis 3:21
17. John 3:16; Hebrews 13:20
18. Exodus 25, Leviticus 16, and Hebrews 9.
19. John 3:16
20. I Peter 1:18
21. Hebrews 9:22

Chapter 5

1. Exodus 20:7
2. Proverbs 30:4 KJV
3. Isaiah 42:8 (literal)
4. Exodus 3:15 NIV
5. John 17:6, 26
6. Psalms 22:22 KJV
7. Psalm 103:1 (literal)
8. Psalms 8:1 (literal)
9. Psalms 34:3
10. Psalms 68:4 (literal)
11. Song of Solomon 1:3 KJV
12. Psalms 5:11 KJV
13. Deuteronomy 32:2-3 literal

Notes

Chapter 6
1. II Corinthian 5:19-20
2. Nineteenth century hymn, "Holy, Holy, Holy," by Reginald Heber and John B. Dykes
3. Isaiah 53:5, 7, 11
4. John 3:16
5. Hymn, "Amazing Grace," by John Newton, 1779.

Chapter 7
1. Genesis 15:1
2. Genesis 15:6
3. Romans 4:23-25
4. Ephesians 2:8-9
5. Exodus 12
6. Luke 23:42-43
7. Acts 2:37-38
8. Acts 10:24-48
9. Acts 16:30-31
10. Joel 2:32 NIV

Chapter 8
1. Hebrews 10:16
2. II Corinthians 5:17
3. I Corinthians 6:17
4. I Corinthians 6:19
5. Colossians 1:27
6. Galatians 2:20 KJV
7. John 14:16-17
8. Hebrews 13:5 KJV
9. John 14:17
10. Acts 1:8
11. Galatians 5:22-23
12. I Thessalonians 5:19

Chapter 9
1. I Corinthians 2:9
2. John 17:24
3. John 14:2-3 KJV
4. Revelation 21:27
5. Revelation 19:16
6. Revelation 5:9-10
7. Revelation 5:13
8. Acts 1:9-11
9. Zechariah 12:1,2,3

10. Luke 21:27-28
11. I Thessalonians 4:15-18
12. Titus 2:13-14
13. Romans 8:24-25

Chapter 10

1. Matthew 27:51
2. John 14:6
3. Hebrews 11:6

Chapter 11

1. II Corinthians 5:14,15
2. Hebrews 12:28
3. Romans 11:22
4. Luke 14:27,33
5. John 6:28-29
6. I John 3:23
7. Romans 13:8-10
8. Hebrews 10:25
9. Acts 20:29
10. Galatians 5:13 NIV

Chapter 12

1. Proverbs 16:32
2. I Peter 2:11
3. Galatians 5:17
4. Romans 6:11
5. Romans 7:24-25
6. Ephesians 6:12
7. I John 5:4
8. Revelation 12:11

Appendix I

1. Romans 1:19-20; Psalms 19:1-4
2. Psalms 14:1
3. I John 4:8
4. John 14:9
5. Deuteronomy 6:4
6. Genesis 1:26
7. John 10:30
8. Ephesians 2:7
9. I John 5:11

Notes

10. Atharva Veda X:10
11. Hebrews 9:27
12. Hebrews 10:10
13. I Corinthians 15:17,19-20,21-22
14. Proverbs 3:5-6
15. Revelation 21:1
16. II Peter 3:10
17. Isaiah 30:26
18. Joel 2:31
19. Matthew 24:29
20. Matthew 24:33
21. I Peter 2:11
22. I John 1:9
23. I John 1:7

Appendix II

1. Exodus 25:22
2. II Samuel 6:7
3. Genesis 5:24
4. II Kings 2:11
5. Revelation 11:19
6. Hebrews 13:20

Epilogue

1. Luke 18:17
2. John 18:38
3. John 14:6

Editing note: Style varies with the capitalization of pronouns referring to deity. Some Bible translations capitalize, and some do not. Most other writings do. We decided to capitalize, but the reader will notice scriptural quotes that do not. We had to show the quotes accurately. This explains what may appear as an inconsistency.

Special Notice To Reader

Your comments on this book would be greatly appreciated. Please complete the following, tear out (or use separate sheet), and forward to the address below.

Did the book increase your understanding? _____

Did it affect your life? _____

How? _____

Other comments? _____

_____
Use additional sheets if necessary

Your name _____ Telephone (____) _____

Street _____ Apt # _____

City _____ State _____ Zip _____

Send your comments to:
CREATIVE PUBLISHERS ☐ P. O. Box 61431 ☐ Virginia Beach, VA 23462

HERE'S A GREAT IDEA FOR YOU!

If this book helped you understand truth and the meaning of life, we urge you to be a blessing to others. Share the book with friends and relatives. Also, we strongly recommend widespread use of the book as the perfect gift item. The price of the book puts it in a reasonable price range for a gift. It enables you to share "The World's Greatest Truths" with friends and loved ones in a unique and entertaining way! You will be giving a gift that may have unimaginable benefit. The recipient will find it attractive and fascinating, and will probably always be grateful. Order gift copies today for birthdays, weddings, anniversaries, graduations, Christmas, and other special occasions, or just "thinking of you" situations as a surprise gift.

Purchase or order where you bought this book, or order directly to the address above. If you order direct from the publisher's address above, the following prices apply (subject to change without notice):

    1 to 5 copies: $12.95   over 5 copies: $11.66 each (10% discount)

Add $2.50 per order for shipping and handling. In Virginia, add 4.5% sales tax.

Order now!